THE PROBLEM
WITH POETRY

Open University Press

English, Language, and Education series
General Editor: Anthony Adams
Lecturer in Education, University of Cambridge

TITLES IN THE SERIES

Narrative and Argument
Richard Andrews (ed.)

The Problem with Poetry
Richard Andrews

Time for Drama
Roma Burgess and Pamela Gaudry

Computers and Literacy
Daniel Chandler and Stephen Marcus (eds)

Readers, Texts, Teachers
Bill Corcoran and Emrys Evans (eds)

Thinking Through English
Paddy Creber

Developing Response to Poetry
Patrick Dias and Michael Hayhoe

Developing English
Peter Dougill (ed.)

The Primary Language Book
Peter Dougill and Richard Knott

Children Talk About Books
Donald Fry

Literary Theory and English Teaching
Peter Griffith

Lesbian and Gay Issues in the English Classroom
Simon Harris

Reading and Response
Mike Hayhoe and Stephen Parker (eds)

Assessing English
Brian Johnston

Lipservice: The Story of Talk in Schools
Pat Jones

The English Department in a Changing World
Richard Knott

Oracy Matters
Margaret MacLure, Terry Phillips, and Andrew Wilkinson (eds)

Language Awareness for Teachers
Bill Mittins

Beginning Writing
John Nicholls *et al.*

Teaching Literature for Examinations
Robert Protherough

Developing Response to Fiction
Robert Protherough

Microcomputers and the Language Arts
Brent Robinson

English Teaching from A–Z
Wayne Sawyer, Anthony Adams and Ken Watson

Reconstructing 'A' Level English
Patrick Scott

School Writing
Yanina Sheeran and Douglas Barnes

Reading Narrative as Literature
Andrew Stibbs

Collaboration and Writing
Morag Styles (ed.)

Reading Within and Beyond the Classroom
Dan Taverner

Reading for Real
Barrie Wade (ed.)

English Teaching in Perspective
Ken Watson

The Quality of Writing
Andrew Wilkinson

The Writing of Writing
Andrew Wilkinson (ed.)

Spoken English Illuminated
Andrew Wilkinson, Alan Davies and Deborah Berrill

THE PROBLEM WITH POETRY

Richard Andrews

Open University Press
Milton Keynes · Philadelphia

Open University Press
Celtic Court
22 Ballmoor
Buckingham
MK18 1XW

and
1900 Frost Road, Suite 101
Bristol, PA 19007, USA

First Published 1991

British Library Cataloguing in Publication Data

Andrews, Richard
  The problem with poetry. – (English language, and education series)
  1. Poetry
  I. Title   II. Series
  808.1

  ISBN 0-335-09339-6

Library of Congress Cataloging-in-Publication Data

Andrews, Richard, 1953–
    The problem with poetry/Richard Andrews.
      p.   cm.—(English, language, and education series)
    Includes bibliographical references and index.
    ISBN 0-335-09339-6
    1. English poetry—Study and teaching.   2. Poetry—Study and
  teaching.   I. Title.   II. Series.
  PR504.5.A5   1991
  808.1'07—dc20
                                                        90-21424
                                                          CIP

Typeset by Rowland Phototypesetting Ltd
Bury St Edmunds, Suffolk
Printed in Great Britain by Biddles Ltd
Guildford and King's Lynn

for
Robert Protherough

il miglior docente

Contents

General editor's introduction

Richard Andrews will already be known to readers of this series through his earlier edited book, *Narrative and Argument*. In *The Problem with Poetry* he continues his exploration of genre and focuses upon the received notion that the teaching of poetry is, for many teachers at least, problematical, as Richard himself points out in the first chapter. My own experience of teaching poetry to secondary pupils would lead me to conclude that the 'problems' are more of the teacher's own making than ones that exist in the minds of the students. I have found few elements within the English curriculum more rewarding and (at least in some senses of the word) 'easier' to teach than poetry. It can indeed, and does, 'speak for itself'. But this is clearly not the universal experience of English classrooms: it is all too common for my students on teaching practice to be asked by the regular class teacher to 'do some poetry with the class as we have not got round to it yet this year'. Richard Andrews has, then, done us all a service by his clear analysis of why these problems exist and his attempts to show some of the ways in which they may be surmounted.

There is much practicality here (especially in the later chapters) that the classroom teacher will be able to put into instant action. Yet the book goes far beyond this. It is based upon a clear conception of the nature of the genre and a mere glance at the bibliography will demonstrate the wealth of scholarship on which it depends. Reading through the first draft was for me like coming face-to-face with old friends, some of whom had been long forgotten, such as the reference to Ezra Pound and Ernest Fenollosa, an essay I found of especial help when, as a graduate student, I was beginning to grapple with the 'problems' that Andrews analyses so cogently. For this reader at least, the present volume marks the latest stage on a quest for understanding that began in undergraduate days.

A letter to hand from the publisher as I prepare this introduction quotes Wallace Stevens as saying, 'Poetry is a response to the daily necessity of getting the world right'. This seems to me to contain profound truth and to make it all the more necessary, within our increasingly enterprise-dominated curriculum, to give poetry its true weight and significance. Readers in England and Wales may share my anxiety that, in the new National Curriculum for English, poetry may be marginalized in spite of the references to Wordsworth and others in the Report of Professor Brian Cox's Working Group. Part of the problem, I suspect, is that teachers are not only insecure about how to teach poetry but are uncertain what, in fact, they should teach. One wonders how many teachers of English are themselves regular readers of poetry, especially that poetry which is being written anew and restoring again the essential power of the language of the tribe.

Paradoxically the hunger for poetry is evident all around us. It can be seen in the 'verses' on Christmas and birthday cards, in popular song, in local newspapers, in some of the more imaginative of television advertisements. The sense of fun with words, discussed especially in Chapter 7 (it is good to see an extended exploration here of the work of Edwin Morgan), may only be a starting point for an endless journey of discovery but it is a vitally important one for many children, and many of their parents also. It is a mark of the skilled argument of this book that it moves from the deceptively simple to the seemingly complex with equal authority within a few pages.

The rehabilitation of poetry in the secondary English curriculum (it had never really lost its role in most primary schools) probably began with the publication in 1987 of *Teaching Poetry in the Secondary School: An HMI View* to which Richard Andrews makes appropriate reference. It is interesting that this publication was one year earlier than the Kingman Report, *An Inquiry into the Teaching of English*, an apparently very different document. Yet we cannot really have one without the other: poetry is language, and language, poetry. The rehabilitation seems to me one that is much needed in the present climate when curriculum issues can be all too easily polarized.

The present book is itself a major statement in this process of rehabilitation and one that deserves to be discussed as a scholarly contribution to a continual debate in its own right as well as a skilled assembly of views and practices.

Readers will no doubt note that the book is dedicated to Richard's colleague at the University of Hull, Robert Protherough, himself a distinguished contributor to this series. By the time this book is published Robert will have retired from his university post. I know that Richard wanted the present volume to stand as, in some ways, a tribute to Protherough's work and contribution to English teaching. As the series' General Editor, I would very much wish to associate myself with these sentiments.

Anthony Adams

Acknowledgements

Much of the inspiration for this book has come from working with primary and secondary students in Britain and Hong Kong, and with teachers both there and in New York. I would particularly like to thank Janie Lai, Jong-hay Rha, Lauren Wu, Daniel Green, Helen Cooper and Parisjat Banomyong of Island School, Hong Kong; Mary and Martin Keegan, Keith Vyas, Thomas O'pray and Vincent Lee and their headteacher, Ruth Crow, at Millbank School, London; Carmel Christian of St John Bosco School (now Cardinal Heenan High School), Leeds; Rachel Allen of Joseph Rowntree School, York; and Matthew Dalton and Stephen Taylor of The Cedars Upper School and Community College, Leighton Buzzard for the inclusion of their poems. I am also grateful to Edwin Morgan for granting permission for his poems to be included, and for the kind attention he has shown on many occasions; to Harriet Bailer and Susan Di Carlo; and to David Homer, Jacqui Cook and Helen Nixon of the South Australian College of Advanced Education for the use of their material. Many thanks also to Pam McEwen and the International Reading Association for permission to reprint 'Super Bowl XXII'; to Anvil Press Poetry; to Help the Aged, to Roger Knight of *The Use of English*, and to Hilary Minns and the editorial committee of *English in Education* for permission to include reworkings of articles that originally appeared in those journals.

Several friends and colleagues have helped me along the way: in particular, I am indebted to Angela Fisher, Penny Willis, Bob Smeaton, Peter Medway, Kingsley Ervin, Ian Bentley, Monique Pirie and, especially, Dodi Beardshaw; to Richard Sterling and Carla Asher for asking me to run a course on poetry at the New York City Writing Project's 1990 summer school, and to the teachers on that course who inspired me to look again at some of my assumptions; to Anthony Adams, John Skelton and Bobbi Whitcombe for their support, encouragement and editorial vision. Finally, I wish to acknowledge the debt I owe to Robert Protherough. With all its shortcomings – which are mine own – it is to him that the book is dedicated.

The author has made every effort to contact copyright holders, but in some cases this has not proved possible. The publishers would be glad to hear from any further copyright owners of material reproduced in *The Problem with Poetry*.

1 The problem(s)

You could object that by titling a book *The Problem with Poetry*, I am creating problems where there are none; that it would be far better to assume there were no problems, to let poetry 'speak for itself' and to call the book something like *The Joy in Poetry* or *Poetry for Pleasure*.

It seems better to face up to the fact that many teachers and pupils do find poetry problematic. As this is a book for teachers rather than pupils, we can weigh the pleasures, revelations and power of poetry against the problems that teachers and pupils face in reading and writing it. Poetry seems to have this paradoxical nature: it is both energizing and 'difficult', revealing and cryptic at the same time. Perhaps that in itself is part of the problem?

And perhaps it is a case of the *problems* with poetry rather than a single problem. There seem to be at least seven problems associated with the writing, reading and teaching of poetry. Each of these will be discussed and some tentative solutions offered in the rest of the book.

Definition

Once, as a teaching student, I witnessed a lesson in which a teacher lit sparklers in front of a class of Year 8 children, passed some around the class and then urged everyone to 'write a poem'. The experience generated a great deal of excitement, but then a hush spread around the room. I overheard one girl say to her friend, 'What *is* a poem?'. This question has remained an important one for me in thinking about what we ask children to do in class, and in the assumptions we make about literary form. It is a question that seems little to do with the experience of seeing, hearing, smelling, touching (and in the case of one child, tasting) the sparklers, and everything to do with the shaping of what the child had to say.

Coming up with an abstract definition of a poem would have been of no help at the time: what the child needed was some guidance as to how to lay out her words on the page. Being aware of the nature and limits of the poem as a teacher would

2 THE PROBLEM WITH POETRY

inform a reaction to such a question. I discuss various definitions of 'poem' in Chapter 2.

'Not poetry!'

Along with 'Shakespeare' and 'old-fashioned comprehension' (i.e. a decontextualized passage plus questions), poetry seems to get the most groans from pupils when it is introduced in class. Why is this? Could it be that the perceived 'difficulties' of poetry are off-putting, or that the voice that often seems to be found for poetry when it is read aloud or recited is too remote, too precious to provoke anything but giggles and derision? Is it the ambiguities of poetry, the sense that you can't always pin down what the writer is saying, and that readings slip through your fingers like water: you can't be sure of what is being said? Are these some of the factors that account for the fact that poetry is not widely read – nothing like as widely as novels or newspapers?

Surveys into the voluntary reading of poetry only serve to confirm these impressions. Jenkinson (1940) in a study in the late 1930s observed 'the unyielding resistance to the appeals of poetry' and deplored the unsuitable diet of poetry which schools offered to children. Yarlott and Harpin (1970–1: p. 96) writing at the end of the sixties note:

> In recent years the range of poetry offered has increased immensely, modern anthologies have a welcome physical attractiveness for the reader and yet, as we see from a comparison of Jenkinson's figures with ours, the bedrock of resistance to poetry among boys endures virtually unchanged, nor is it negligible among girls except at A level.

Of the 800 O Level candidates surveyed in 1968, only one in eight showed any marked desire to continue reading poetry after leaving school; the investigators concluded that 16-year-olds' attitude to poetry was largely one of indifference and dislike. Their implied recommendation, however, is somewhat dismissive in itself:

> One is bound to ask therefore whether the examining boards should continue to demand a study of poetry as a compulsory element in the O level examination . . . For the majority of fourth and fifth years it might be better if the study of poetry were made a voluntary or occasional rather than a compulsory activity.

Part of the problem might be that teachers, like any other member of society, do not read much poetry. Poetry has a small but committed audience in this country. Initial print-runs of new books of poems are low, except for books by the giants.

And of course, poetry suffers as perhaps the 'highest' literary form from attitudes that extol the 'realistic' at the expense of the 'fictional'. It is seen as the most distant from 'everyday life', as the least 'useful' of the arts, as inhabiting an enclosed, self-referential world to which only an élite gain access. Furthermore, it has acquired associations of 'wetness' in our narrowly masculine view of what is important in society.

All these prejudices about poetry are hard – but not impossible – to break down. The reasons for these various but connected attitudes towards poetry will be examined in Chapter 2, and practical approaches to deal with the antipathy to poetry will be presented in the second half of the book.

Form and structure

Poems are relatively short. This could be seen as a positive advantage in a school or anywhere, but often the brevity of poems can cause problems. Whereas novels and short stories are long enough to keep children quiet for at least twenty minutes, poems end after a minute (often less). You read them a second time, or ask pupils to read then again, slowly. There is still forty-five minutes to go before the end of the session. You read another. Then you find a narrative poem. This takes two minutes, but still you are left with a gaping chasm of time to fill.

Not only are they short, but they also seem to be written in a foreign language. This isn't the language of speech or even of prose.

Then there is the technical language *about* poetry: poems come in such a variety of shapes and sizes and draw on a large range of rhetorical devices that in order to gain command of the field, you think you need to have a reference guide to help you. Sonnets, haiku and tanka, quatrains, tercets and terza rima are bad enough; then you have to grapple with simile and metaphor (the straws that drowning teachers hang on to), and worse, with synedoche, personification and caesuras.

Much of the problem here is to do with poetry's identification with rhythm. It is rhythm that might be seen as the key to the nature of poetry and to an understanding of the place of poetry in the world of discourse; but the language to describe rhythm in our culture is limited. That in itself is another problem, as Forrest-Thomson (1978) and others have recognized.

The problems of form, poetic language, the technical language about poetry and the language of rhythm will form the focus of Chapter 4.

The range of poetry

A large proportion of the poetry 'done' in schools comes from a rich but narrow tradition. This is the 'English canon' that runs from the mid-sixteenth century to the present, which largely consists of male poets and lyrical poems to be read in reflective (often melancholy) mood. This canon is mediated to children through anthologies, by far the most likely place for children to find poems in school. The anthologies themselves fall into various categories, and their contents are arranged in various ways (e.g. by theme, author or chronologically).

This unofficial canon represents a particular poetic. It sees poetry as standing in a rather secluded place in the range of social discourses: to exaggerate the case slightly, poetry is for reading in private; it is about the self and its quest for awareness; it is about feeling as opposed to thought; about reflection as opposed to action; drawing on imagination rather than on reason.

This poetic causes problems that have much in common with those identified above. Chapter 5 looks at the range of poetry used and available, and at ways of extending the range to include writing from the whole world (including writing by women!). The problem of translation – so often erected as a barrier to the appreciation of poems in other languages, and yet one we must address if we are to extend the horizons of poetry in our schools – is addressed in Chapter 4 via two poems by Baudelaire.

The way poetry is taught

It could be that one of the problems with poetry is not so much part of poetry's problem (or with attitudes towards it) but the use to which it is put in schools. Consider the following scenarios:

— a teacher, dissatisfied with the way a child is reading aloud a poem to the class, takes over the reading to gain the full effect of the poem;
— a teacher 'explains' the poem to the children who don't see the connections and significances that the teacher sees in the text;
— a school in which there is no connection made between the lyrics of popular culture and the lyric poetry of written cultures.

In each case, the poem is appropriated by the teacher who disowns the pupil. The children feel that their own voices are not worthy of inheriting the enshrined voices of literature, and so, quite understandably, they take no further interest in them.

This is a general problem with teaching technique, rather than one specific to poetry. But because poetry is seen, rightly or wrongly, as the pinnacle of literary achievement, the resentment on the part of the pupils is all the greater: they are expected to enjoy the text, so when they don't the sense of failure all round is considerable. There almost comes with poetry a moral obligation to enjoy it.

In the companion volume to this one in the 'English, Language and Education' series – a book focusing on response rather than on production – Patrick Dias and Mike Hayhoe (1988) identify the critical theory implicit in much teaching of poetry in secondary schools as 'a prime cause' of the unpopularity of poetry in the classroom. They refer to three post-war movements in critical theory: New Criticism, with its emphasis on 'close reading', the 'unity' of the text, the primacy of the poem as critical fodder and its devaluation of the role of the reader; Structuralism and systematic poetics (pp. 13–14), the consequence of which is a curriculum

> within which literature is no longer to be privileged, but is one mode of discourse among other discourse systems;

and post-structuralist positions which are more reader-centred and which focus on the interaction between reader and text. It has to be said that if their book sets up its camp in the third of these fields, this one is in the second.

The problem of teaching approach is not only confined to literature: it is part of a more general disowning of voice that is still endemic to schooling and which is gradually changing as our awareness of the value of talk and expression changes.

Poetry and assessment

Many of the disempowering approaches to the teaching of poetry described above are the result of having to teach within the requirements of an assessment system. Indeed, Margaret Mathieson, in an article entitled 'The Problem of Poetry' (Mathieson 1980) takes this as her principal problem. On the one hand, poems are ideal for assessment (and particularly examination) purposes, and consequently they are often used, not only in literature assessments but also in 'language' papers (perhaps because they are assumed to be the 'best words in the best order'). On the other hand, they can give up their meanings more reluctantly and/or more ambivalently than prose, which complicates the examining process. They have an advantage (or perhaps the misfortune, whichever way you look at it) of being short enough to be included as a whole text in a paper or as the basis for coursework.

Mathieson's objection centres on the feeling that 'inappropriate academic demands force analysis' upon teachers (p. 38), and that this is 'entirely unsuitable as an approach to poetry for the great majority'. And so follows the irony that while 'examinations ensure that poetry continues to be taught, they do so in such a way that few derive much satisfaction from it.' (p. 40).

This is a double irony, because the freeing of poetry from the shackles of examinations would (indeed, will) free teachers from the responsibility of having to 'do' poetry at all.

Poetry and the National Curriculum

I include this section in the review of problems with poetry because it seems to me that the place of poetry in the national curriculum is not as assured as it might be.

Despite the credo-like nature of *Teaching Poetry in the Secondary School*, the HMI booklet published in 1987, government-sponsored reports and proposals seem not to know what to do with poetry. The Bullock Report, *A Language for Life* (DES 1975), devotes eight paragraphs to it. The attitude of indifference to poetry is recorded; poetry 'is either numinous, and therefore rarely to be invoked, or an object of comic derision' (9.22). But the report offers little in the way of a solution to this problem. Its attitude towards definition is cavalier and conservative:

> Definitions of poetry are almost limitless, but they always agree upon this central fact: that it is a man speaking to men [sic], of his and their condition, in a language which consists of the best words in the best order.

As we will see in the following chapter, it is simply untrue that definitions of poetry 'always agree upon this central fact'; and, apart from the fact that women seem to be left out of the equation, the notion of 'the best words in the best order' is general enough to apply to a whole range of discourses.

Following the research of Yarlott and Harpin already cited in this chapter, the report concludes that:

> It is clear to us that this antipathy [to poetry] rests substantially in the *method* of teaching it

especially in the old-fashioned comprehension approach.

The Kingman Report (DES 1988: p. 38) mentions poetry lessons only as evidence of learning about language. There is a recommendation to pay attention to form, but a note of regret that 'much that is valuable has been lost' in the abandoning of conventional metrical forms in writing:

> Both professional poets and tentative beginners can be led to felicitous discoveries of new words and phrases (and even thoughts) by the exigencies of rhyme. Real poems often begin with a cadence or a form, before the 'content' is known at all.

Cox (DES 1989) is both encouraging and limiting. Within the proposed attainment targets for Speech and Listening and for Reading (ATs 1 and 2), poetry seems to have an assured place. From the start, at levels 1 and 2 of attainment target 1, pupils should be able to 'listen attentively, and respond, to stories and poems; and at higher levels, should be able to talk about differences between forms and genres of writing, both at the generic level between poetry and other forms of discourse, and at the formal level between different kinds of poetry. The emphasis on an international range of poetry is encouraging too, and on exploring pre-twentieth century works. In the earlier set of proposals for the 5–11 age range, there is the added dimension that 'children should be encouraged to explore poetry through discussion, *imitation* and through a wide range of activities' (my italics).

David Garnett (1989), in responding to the Cox Report, traces the chain of anxiety about poetry that runs from Arnold through Zimmerman to Strong and the official government reports of the sixties and seventies: the sense that poetry is important – indeed 'central' – to the curriculum, but the accompanying sense of disappointment that it is not loved by the majority of children who are on the receiving end of it. He also unearths a 1985 article by Cox which declares:

> I would give up most of my literary criticism work, and make a long serious effort to learn the craft of verse . . . At school itself the teaching of the verbal arts should be compulsory at all levels, and this should continue in higher education;

and where it is clear that the individual-centred, sense-centred and imagination-based creative writing movement needs the interaction with texts from cultural traditions in order to be of lasting value. This is a balanced, potentially fruitful position to take: one which combines the workshop approach (with children making poems) with the more well-established practices of reading, performing and discussing poetry.

David Preen (1990: p. 30) is less enthusiastic and less hopeful. He sees the treatment of poetry and of poetic language in the report as 'simply skeletal', and the lack of a discussion of 'the great coral reef made of metaphor and symbol' as inexcusable. There is no sense of the transformational power of poetic language, and even in a report which flirts with 'modes' of language or one that builds upon the model of language offered in Kingman, no real sense of poetry as a distinctive kind of discourse.

And there is a caveat in the Cox Report (17.29) itself which has an ominous ring to it – one that echoes earlier reservations about poetry:

> We believe that, throughout the school years, all children should have ample opportunities to write poetry, either singly or in groups; this is made explicit in the programmes of study. However, we have not included a poetry strand in the statements of attainment because we do not feel that any pupil should be *required* to write a poem in order to achieve a particular level of attainment.[1]

This can be read as advantageous to poetry in one sense. To be freed from the statements of attainment is a blessing, as all too often we have seen poetry – as text to be read – used as fodder for examination and assessment purposes. In another sense, however, it might consign poetry (temporarily, we must hope) to oblivion: if no one is going to be required to write poetry, few teachers will try it. Under the pressure of fulfilling attainment targets and assessment requirements, the branch of poetry might wither. Part of the purpose of the present book is to argue the case for the writing of poetry alongside the reading and discussing of it as a practice beneficial to all children. Without it, the language arts are seriously impoverished.

Note

1 Within this limitation, the statutory orders are positive enough: 'Pupils should have the opportunities to write poetry (individually, in small groups or as a class) and to experiment with different layouts, rhymes, rhythms, verse structures and with all kinds of sound effects and verbal play.' (KS 2 programme of study, para. 18).

2 What is a poem?

> A poem is a collection of words which do not go right up to the edge of
> the paper.
>
> Year 7 pupil

It is important to try and define what we mean by 'poem', not only because there is a good deal of overlap and confusion between the terms 'poem', 'poetry', 'poetic', 'poetics' and 'verse', but also because we need to be sure of our ground when we discuss poems with students (especially when we compare them to other forms of discourse) and when we are arguing the case for poetry in the curriculum.

Some of the best definitions of 'poem' come from classes of 11–12 year olds at North Walsham New High School, reported by Ray Tarleton in his article 'Children's thinking and poetry' (1983: p. 37). Tarleton asked four Year 7 English groups (over a hundred children) how they would explain what a poem was to a Martian. Predictable responses were preoccupied with the surface features of poems: verses and rhyme, punctuation and capital letters:

> Pupils saw the process of writing as mechanical, dull and forced – a process of
> construction, not a process of creation: words are 'cleverly' put together into
> grammatical and rhyming patterns. The range of subjects they thought poems could
> deal with was limited, and bound by convention: 'the seasons changing, flowers in
> spring, animals and many other things that are beautiful'. Poems were seen as mainly
> descriptive.

The more original responses, however, considered structure and form at more essential levels. Here are some of them:

A poem is a collection of words which do not go right up to the edge of the paper
A sort of story which is set down ways
Thoughts displayed in rhythmic pattern
A sort of rhythmic story
A poem is a song with no music
A sort of song that shows the poet's feeling

The striking element in these definitions is the emphasis on *form*. The first is a delightfully apposite definition which fits many more poems than some of the functional and much vaguer definitions offered by adult writers. It is true that if you hold up a poem and look at it from a distance (far enough so that you can no longer identify the individual words), you can still see that it is a poem by its layout on the page. The layout is deliberate and purposeful; it is a visual equivalent of a rhythmic pattern.

Two of the definitions focus on the rhythmic quality in poetry, and we shall return to this topic in Chapter 4. For the present, it is worth looking at what else is contained in these two definitions. First, there is the notion of 'thoughts', which is encouraging when the assumption might be that children (and adults) associate poetry only with the expression of feeling.

Second, there is the notion of 'display', which discourse theorists would be delighted to see in the definition ('display texts' are not like everyday interactive discourse, like conversation; they 'hold court').

Third is the notion of 'pattern', a borrowing from the visual world but here applied to the aural.

Fourth, in the second definition, is the association with 'story'. Here, narratologists would delight in the classing of 'poem' (which in our culture is predominantly lyric) with story and narrative. Another definition in the list ('A sort of story which is set down ways') marvellously captures this connection.

But let this connection not obscure the distinction between narrative and lyric. A 'story' – as a particular kind of narrative – works in relation to chronological, sequential, 'linear' time. It may play with chronology, reversing the order of 'events' for particular effects, moving backwards and forwards in time and almost certainly selecting moments in time to present as the story. A lyric works differently in relation to linear time. It is not 'atemporal', as Culler (1975) suggests, but 'supra-temporal'. That is to say, it uses rhythmic patterning to 'defeat' time, to reach a state of sublimity or to create the effect of an 'eternal present'. This is the state that may also become the theme of some poems – and indeed, it is characteristic of poetry to explore this particular theme. But we must not forget that this 'supra-temporality' is created with temporal elements. It is the arrangement of the lines as rhythmic units which create the patterns of expectation, paralleling and comparability both within lines and in the stanzas or sections of the poem, and in the poem as a whole. Associations of 'universality', ambiguity and timelessness are built on this basis.

The remaining two definitions forge a connection with song, and the first of these ('a song with no music') is particularly interesting. Stripping a song of its music (i.e. its melody, intonation) would seem to leave us with nothing but the words (the 'lyrics'); but there is a residual element that song and poetry share, viz. rhythm.

A minority of Ray Tarleton's children focused on the freedoms that come with poetry:

There are not many rules to poems
You can write down all your feelings not bothering with sentences
A poem can be what you want it to be
A poem can be about anything. They can help you

While acknowledging the impracticality of 'a poem can be what you want it to be', there is a liberating magic about this definition. Perhaps only story has the same power. And if children see this textual arena as one in which they are totally empowered, in which there are no limitations and 'not many rules', what an important arena it is to preserve and fight for. Note that 'you can write down all your feelings *not bothering with sentences*'. Is the sentence antipathetic to poetry? Does the sentence conspire against the free expression of thoughts and feelings? Of course, most poems still operate in sentences; working across the structure and momentum of the sentence, in most cases, are the cross rhythms that establish the musical dimension of the poem. And the tensions created produce some of the particular pleasures of poetry. In the following poem by a thirteen-year-old, punctuation – in the conventional sense as used in prose – is absent until the last three lines. Then the full-stop after 'lips' holds up the momentum and rhythm of the poem for a split second longer than has been the case, and the final couplet (after the more langorous build-up of the words ending with the suffix -*ness*) is alive with pace and pregnant with closure:

Spring

Spring is
The softness of a cat's fur
The madness
In the round eyes of a cat
The sleepiness
Hanging round the cat's closed lips.
The animation
Running on the cat's whiskers.
(Jong-hay Rha)

This experimentation with language is important for a number of reasons. It allows writers to play with the shape of the sentence, to emphasize phrasing, to use punctuation as a secondary form of notation, to seek out repetitions in the structure of language that will add to the overall effect of what is being said and to give particular words and phrases the status of a line to themselves. At the same time, questions arise like 'Should I start each new line with a capital letter?'. This question may seem of little import, but it is actually one worth pursuing with children. What difference would it make to 'Spring' if the convention of starting new lines with a capital letter was abandoned?

Spring is
the softness of a cat's fur
the madness
in the round eyes of a cat
the sleepiness
hanging round the cat's closed lips.
The animation
running on the cat's whiskers.

Such a question can also be tested by rewriting a few lines of Shakespeare in this way. Does it lend a little more weight to the claims of sentence structure – and thus make it easier to read – than to those of the iambic pentameter?

Tarleton also notes that the more predictable responses see 'description' as a *sine qua non* of the poem: 'it has got to have descriptions', '. . . adjectives'. This adjectival insistence is intriguing. It is associated with a particular kind of poetry, a kind which is indeed common in our culture. This poetry is static, moody and contrived. It finds realization in the approach to writing in schools where words are listed on the board before the act of writing is permitted: 'spooky words' or 'sad words', for example.

In answer to the question 'What might a poem contain?', Tarleton records that various subjects were suggested, ranging from the predictable 'places, flowers, winter, summer, autumn and spring' to 'religion, murder and truth'. Poems could be 'funny, sad, about childhood, about sex, about violence, about drugs, about suicide, murder, sorrow, nature or anything' (p. 40). One response had

> Nonsense fiction fact non fiction big words excitement beat rudeness rhythm serious hilarious boring pathetic disgusting gory comparisons exclamation marks and things pictures round the side.

Further definitions

One superb double definition appears in Ted Hughes' introduction to his anthology *Here Today* (1963). One the one hand, he talks of explosive 'compression' as 'one of the first virtues of poetry'. This in itself indicates something of the reading experience – the 'explosion' of meaning that we experience at the unpacking or release of the compression – and as such is not limited to poetry. A Hemingway or Raymond Carver story might be similarly described. On the other hand, Hughes talks about a 'dance in words' (pp. 11–12):

> [The poet] can be excited by countless varied feelings. And his inner singing and dancing fit the feelings. But because he is a poet, and full of words, his song-dance does not break into real song, as it would if he were a musician, or into real dancing, as it would if he were a dancer. It breaks into words. And the dance and the song come out somehow within the words. The dance makes the words move in a pattern, which we call meter and versification. The song makes the sound of the lines rise and fall against each other, which we call the music of poetry, or the cadence.

This second aspect of poetry connects with some of the definitions offered by the Year 7 children earlier: those, in particular, which stress the rhythmic, patterned nature of poetry. The dance metaphor is particularly apt as it embodies both the rhythmic shape in time, and the spatial, choreographic dimension. Taken together with 'explosive compression', 'a dance in words' forms a powerful and comprehensive definition of a poem. The interesting split in the second definition between the dance and the song reflect a similar split in Pound's accounts of the rhythmic nature of poetry. We will explore that distinction further in Chapter 4.

Sylvia Plath, in 'A Comparison' (collected in *Johnny Panic and the Bible of Dreams*, 1977) compares a poem with a novel in terms of its subject matter. 'I have never put a toothbrush in a poem,' she claims. She seems to be suggesting that toothbrushes and other 'familiar, useful and worthy things' don't belong in poems, but it is really the difference between the context of the poem and the context of the novel – i.e. what happens to the toothbrush in a poem as opposed to a novel – that she is talking about. Nevertheless, there is a wry wariness about the exclusiveness of poetry that is remarkable in a poet who does include balloons, milk bottles and turnips in her poems as well as seasons, violence and goddesses.

Donald Davie (1967) makes a useful distinction between the 'diction' of poets who select a vocabulary from the language that they employ for the purposes of poetry, and the 'language' that the more eclectic poets like Shakespeare or Hopkins use. Davie's book, *The Purity of Diction in English Verse*, focuses on the late eighteenth-century poets who, he claims, write using such a diction, but the distinction can be applied to the contemporary situation, not only with regard to the poetry scene but also to the writing of poetry in classrooms. Despite the liberalism and catholicity of the imagination, children's writing can draw on a fairly narrow diction. A short-circuited logic operates when we start with the notion that poetry is 'beautiful' and 'life-enhancing': the next assumption is often that its subject matter had better be safe, aesthetically pleasing in itself and from a stock set. What often follows is that the words chosen to say something about this subject either constitute a tame literary diction and/or sound 'insincere' because they don't bear the imprint of the writer's own voice.

This is not to deny that fine effects are sometimes achieved within this narrow range of poetry, just as they are within the late eighteenth-century. It is simply to suggest that we should try to give children access to a wider range of possibilities in poetry.

This notion of 'purity' and exclusiveness spreads itself beyond the confines of diction to infect the whole body of poetry. It is a confusion of the effect of good poetry with the nature of it. It is there, in its characteristically double-edged form, in a definition quoted in *Not Daffodils Again!* (Calthrop and Ede 1984):

> A poem is a verse or rime made up, by the imaginative treatment of experience expression and hightened [sic] use of language more than ordinary speech.
>
> (Darren, Year 7)

This seems fairly predictable, and not necessarily accurate. In fact, it is hard to pin down a definition of 'poetry'. Robert Druce in *The Eye of Innocence* (1965: p. 23) is clear enough in stating what poetry *isn't* – and it is hard to disagree with his list:

It is not necessarily verse. It is not necessarily rhymed. It is not necessarily metrical. It is certainly not wholly devoted to 'poetic' subjects. It is not bespattered with words which the Oxford English Dictionary identifies as (Poet.)

But when it comes to defining what poetry *is*, there is no clear line. Instead, we are offered a series of examples of poems by schoolchildren that all fall within the central tradition of good creative writing: most are detailed evocations in free verse, rich in imagery and texture.

Part of the problem is that the attempt has been made to define 'poetry' rather than 'poem'. 'Poetry' is much broader than 'poem', not only including all that claim the title 'poem' but referring more widely than that to embrace anything with certain *qualities* of poems: a footballer's run with the ball can be described as 'pure poetry'; a splendid pile of profiteroles; an exquisite dance routine. All these draw on one or two qualities assumed to be the essence of poems: beauty, for example, or a kind of distillation of experience.

The term 'poetic' is narrower in range, but still wider than 'poem'. It's a rich and complicated term, referring at once to a particular function of language (see the discussion of Britton's 'poetic' function in Chapter 3), to anything touchingly or sensationally romantic; and, as a noun, to a literary/linguistic system, a kind of semiotic (*The Poetics of Prose, The New Poetic*): note here that it doesn't confine itself in application to poetry, but stretches beyond poetry to literature, and beyond language altogether to refer to engine design, fashion or wrestling.[1]

If 'poem' is conflated with all these related terms, it is bound to take on board some of their freer associations. In a sense, they are metaphors of this basic term 'poem': we need to look again at the original term itself, and try to make positive definitions of it. Furthermore, it seems that the whole picture has been complicated by the fact that many definitions of poetry aim to pin down its (assumed) processes, effects and functions rather than to secure a descriptive basis for those effects. It is rather like trying to pin down vapour, and the result is that the definitions can be applied to other forms of discourse than poetry. Others, like Auden (1963) and Culler (1975), from very different perspectives, question the very attempt to distinguish prose from poetry, or to base a theory of poetry on an account of the special language of poems. With this second proposition I would agree: working at the level of diction, style or subject matter, there is very little to choose between poetry and other forms of discourse. The attempt is doomed to failure because the very level at which the enquiry is taking place – at the level of the poem, i.e. the generic category 'poem' – is not the level at which the distinction is taking place. Thus Culler dismisses Cleanth Brooks' (1947: p. 3) definition of the language of poetry as 'the language of paradox' as applicable to language of any kind, which it is.

Culler would identify poetry 'less with a property of language than with a strategy of reading' (p. 163), and he further details four characteristics of this strategy that we bring to a reading of poetry: these are the fact of distance and impersonality, the expectation of totality or coherence, the notion of thematic

significance and the rhetorical context. But even though he criticizes structural-
ists for not making the point about rhetoric as firmly as they might, Culler fails to
apply these insights about the nature of poetry to the production of it. His stance
is very much one which establishes itself upon the reading of a text, and yet the
generic features and factors which act in symbiotic relationship with the contextual factors outlined above are not explored. Thus we are left with an incomplete
'definition' of a poem, one that is 'reader-centred' but which fails to attribute
enough weight to the text itself.

Other attempts at defining poetry seem to focus on either its supposed effects
or to try and capture its *modus operandi*. Most of these, like 'What was often felt,
but ne'er so well expressed', 'The recollection of emotion in tranquillity' and
'memorable speech' could apply equally to prose, and we can all think of plenty of
examples of poems which don't fit these definitions. And yet these are the
definitions that have informed the sensibility and the responses to poetry. This
kind of definition is useful when we are arguing the case for poetry (as I do in the
last chapter) but not as a description of 'poem' nor as a guide to practice.

It helps to shift the focus to 'poem' rather than 'poetry', and to lay the ghost of
'verse'. The term 'verse' has fallen out of use recently, having been subsumed
within 'poetry'. In many ways, this is a pity, as it offers an interesting set of
dimensions to the description of poems. According to the OED, it can apply not
only to a single line of poetry (derived, as it is, from the Latin *versus* – a line or row
of writing, so named from turning to begin another line), but also to a small
number of metrical lines 'so connected by form or meaning as to constitute either
a work in themselves or a unit in a longer composition', i.e. a stanza. At a higher
level still, it can refer to metrical composition, form or structure as opposed to
prose, and to a body of metrical work as a whole ('The Collected Verse of . . .').
What 'verse' cannot cope with is, ironically, 'free verse'. The new prosodies and
sensibilities required to account for the additive and irregular rhythms of free
verse cannot be included under the umbrella of 'verse', because verse is, by
definition, metrical. 'Poem' is thus the more useful and generally applicable
term because it does cover free and metrical forms, as well as concrete and other
forms. It becomes correspondingly harder to define, however, especially when
flanked by associated terms like 'poetry' and 'poetic' as discussed earlier, and
when plagued by definitions like this from the OED:

> In addition to the metrical or verse form, critics have generally held that in order to
> deserve the name of 'poem', the theme and its treatment must possess qualities
> which raise it above the level of ordinary prose;

or in its condensed version, 'a metrical composition of elevated character'.

Before we try yet another definition of 'poem' let us collect and consider
several examples of poems – a wide range so that our definition is as inclusive as
possible. All of these have been published or declared as poems, though they are
not totally uncontroversial. Indeed, you might want to debate their identity:

1   *ABC*

a b c d e f g
h i j k l m n o p
q r s
t u v
w x y and z
(Traditional)

2   *Speed*

Wheels grinding along the tracks

                             mountain

                      metal   u
                sloping   p
            the   w
        ascending   a
SLOWLY   r
                             d

Steel conveyer belts P U L L I N G   s
    Suddenly . . .
    Swoosh!
          Down
             it
             goes!
                       (Lauren Wu)

3   *A Teacher*

Droning like a fly,
As busy as a bee,
Like a book with no title,
Like a never-ending road;
A never-ending flow of answers.
Like a bad-tempered bear,
Like an unaccomplished writer,
Like a sentence searching for meaning.
An unwritten piece of music,
A table of events,
An eye with no vision,
As sharp as a knife,
And as smart as an owl!
               (Daniel Green)

4   *Advice to a Corkscrew*

(Edwin Morgan)

5   *It's Monday Morning Dad!*

Snort Uuuuuooh.
Snort Uuuuuooh.
tick-tickticktick rinnnng Rrriinnngg.
Err huuu.
hmmmm.
Ermmmm.
huuuu a-cup-tea-would-be-nice, mmmm.
Ermmmm.
Snort Uuuuuooh.
Snort Uuuuuooh.

(Helen Cooper)

6   *Composed upon Westminster Bridge, Sept 3, 1803*

Earth has not anything to shew more fair:
Dull would he be of soul who could pass by
A sight so touching in its majesty:
This city now doth like a garment wear
The beauty of the morning; silent, bare,
Ships, towers, domes, theatres, and temples lie
Open unto the fields, and to the sky;
All bright and glittering in the smokeless air.
Never did sun more beautifully steep
In his first splendour valley, rock, or hill;
Ne'er saw I, never felt, a calm so deep!
The river glideth at his own sweet will:
Dear God! the very houses seem asleep;
And all that mighty heart is lying still!

(William Wordsworth)

7   It was a freezing November night.
I walked along Regent Street against the traffic.

Everyone's arms were filled with presents.
I was heading away from Christmas,
back into October, under the lights.

(Anon)

8   Twas brillig, and the slithy toves
        Did gyre and gimble in the wabe . . .
                    (Lewis Carroll
                from 'Jabberwocky')

What do these texts have in common? What are the elements that combine to enable us to classify them as poems? Perhaps the first point is that, in the words of the Year 7 pupil from Ray Tarleton's class, they 'do not go right up to the edge' of the page.

Second, we can immediately confirm that they do not all rhyme or fall into stanzas or verses; and yet they are all (it is claimed) poems. Some use figurative language and others do not: 'It's Monday Morning Dad!' is clearly not figurative in any way, but rather is a representation of a situation or of character – a kind of vignette. It is also the purest sound poem of the ten, but still a poem all the same. The poem which uses neither simile nor metaphor is [7]; another is William Carlos Williams's 'This is just to say'. We often forget, enmeshed in our poetic of symbols and images, metaphors and similes, that there are poetics and poems which do not work in the same way – some of which consciously eschew this transformational language.

Third, we can say (with the possible exception of [4]) that one principle informing the shape of all of these poems is rhythm, as distinct from metre. Rhythm is more fundamental than metre: its nature is based, in turn, on the principle of repetition, but a repetition that may not be regular. It may be additive and relative, basing its identity on what came before rather than on an underlying regular beat; it may be quantitive, based on syllabic length, or qualitative, based on ictus or stress; it may approximate speech; it may be pointed and reinforced by rhyme or it may not; it may even take the form of metre. But 'rhythm is the original metaphor and encompasses all the others' (Octavio Paz 1974: p. 65). The problem remains regarding [4], however. Unless the term 'rhythm' be stretched metaphorically to apply to space as well as time, it is hard to see 'Advice to a Corkscrew' as rhythmic – though rhythm and design were equated by Ezra Pound in the 'Treatise on Metre': 'Rhythm is a form cut into TIME, as a design is determined SPACE' (1951b: p. 198).

We will return to test the suitability of rhythm as a litmus-test of 'poem' in Chapter 4. I submit it here merely as a hypothesis; but it has to be refined further.

A major objection to this hypothesis is that rhythm is not only the province of poetry. Prose is rhythmic, and so is speech. In fact any utterance that takes up time must, by definition, be rhythmic – and that includes almost all utterances (with the arguable exception of monosyllabic lodestones like the Indian mantra 'om' or 'one-word poems'). The qualification we must add to the rhythmic hypothesis, then, is one that accounts for the heightened or conscious rhythmic shape of the poem. This, more than diction, subject matter, intention, function or surface features like rhyme, punctuation or capital letters at the beginning of lines, is put forward as the single principal determining factor in the definition of 'poem'. It is rhythm which determines layout and form – the *sine qua non* of most poems.

But even this is not sufficient. Although rhythm operates as more of a distinguishing feature than metaphor, it operates within what Genette calls 'that margin of silence'; that is to say, the poem is 'framed' by space on the page or by a shift in tone and/or pace in speech. Both Paz (1974: p. 65) and Auden (1963: p. 58) testify to this ritualistic dimension:

> A poem is a rite; hence its formal and ritualistic character. Its use of language is deliberately and ostentatiously different from talk. Even when it employs the dictions and rhythms of conversation, it employs them as a deliberate informality, presupposing the norm with which they are intended to contrast.

We must take this 'ritualistic' dimension into account when we consider the poem as an art form in the next two chapters.

Note

1 Riffaterre (1978: p. 22) argues this line when he talks about 'poetic discourse' as 'the equivalence established between a word and a text, or a text and another text . . . In all cases the concept of poeticity is inseparable from that of the text. And the reader's perception of what is poetic is based wholly on reference to texts.' This literariness inevitably has repercussions on attitudes to the poem.

3 The poetic

> ... while it is true that poetry often employs words excluded from common usage and has its own special grammar ... it may also happen that poetry uses the same words and the same grammar as everyday language.
>
> M. Riffaterre, *Semiotics of Poetry*

Marjorie Hourd and *The Education of the Poetic Spirit*

Marjorie Hourd's book, published in 1949, drew heavily on theories of imagination and the nature of poetry shaped by Coleridge and then Ruskin. At the same time, it acted as a seminal work – or perhaps a flagship – for the creative writing movement that was to pick up momentum some fifteen years later. In the section of the book devoted to poetry and the imagination (after an opening section on dramatization), she cites Ruskin on the imagination:

> It knows simply what is there, and brings out the positive creature, errorless, unquestionable. So it is throughout art, and in all the imagination does; if anything be wrong it is not the imagination's fault, but some inferior faculty's which would have its foolish say in the matter ... This, however, we need not be amazed at, because the very essence of the imagination is already defined to be the seeing to the heart; and it is not therefore wonderful that it should never err; but it is wonderful, on the other hand, how the composing legalism does *nothing else* than err.
>
> (*Modern Painters*, Vol. III, Ch. XIII, p. 113)

(The 'composing legalism' might best be described as 'forced writing'.) She also refers to Coleridge's famous dictum on the imagination; one that is worth repeating here, if only to lend this side of the argument some weight. Coleridge characterizes imagination as 'that synthetic and magical power' which reveals itself:

> in the balance or reconcilement of opposite or discordant qualities: of sameness, with difference; of the general, with the concrete; the idea, with the image; the individual, with the representative; the sense of novelty and freshness, with old and familiar objects; a more than usual state of emotion, with more than usual order; judgment ever awake and steady self-possession, with enthusiasm and feeling profound or vehement ...
>
> (*Biographia Literaria*, Ch. XIV, ed. by J. Shawcross, Vol. II, p. 12)

One particularly interesting moment in Hourd's analysis of the nine poems by children that are arrayed at the beginning of her discussion is when she turns her attention to a poem with a flawed line in it. This is line four of this opening stanza of a poem called 'Snowdrops':

> Little snowdrops white as snow
> You are so tiny there so low,
> Your little leaves they are so green
> With crinkly lines in between

While from one point of view you might consider it the best line in the stanza (the least clichéd, most observant and detailed in the Ruskinian sense, the closest to the speaking voice), Hourd records how the class objected that 'it isn't true, it's the crocus that has the white lines'. A child was despatched down to the garden to produce a leaf from each plant, and 'in the face of such evidence the line had to be changed' (p. 85). The new line emerged as:

> With crinkly lines and lovely sheen.

But, quite rightly, 'nobody liked the new line, least of all the author'. Hourd's conclusion is that 'had the erroneous fact remained the poem would have been as errorless and unquestionable in its imaginative truth and more perfect in form' (ibid). Thus far I agree; but then she goes on to claim:

> Children can rarely revise with any success at this stage, not in compositions which
> have resulted from such unified acts of the imagination as this one has.

We will look at the drafting of poems in Chapter 6. Suffice it to say here that the revision is not unsatisfactory because it did not form part of the original imaginative conception, but rather that its rhythm (a classic iambic tetrameter) and diction ('lovely sheen') are stilted, and lose the colloquial, conclusive qualities of the original.

A further interesting feature of this exposition is the choice of poems by children. The writers range in age from nearly ten to fifteen (roughly the same as the poems discussed in Chapter 2 of this book), and seem to me quite narrow in formal range. There is a range of imaginative coherence, from the powerfully synthesized to the feebly fanciful, but the narrow subject matter (five on nature, two on the sea, one about dreams and one about love) and the almost relentless dependence on rhymed stanzaic forms (couplets, quatrains and sestets) speaks of a kind of decadence or lack of invention. Admittedly, these limitations are shared by many of the established poets of the Romantic tradition, but it is worth noting that for all the subtle play within those forms, the shape of expressed feeling is remarkably consistent. While part of the programme is a conscious escape from imitation (of the kind represented in Caldwell Cook's *Perse Playbooks*), the very unconscious adoption of these forms has to be seen as something more than imitation: something more like homage or complete immersion in a particular tradition.

In fact, this close association between the writing of a particular tradition and the writing of children is, in another way, something to celebrate, and has always seemed to me one of the great satisfactions of teaching English: that the productions of children are of the same kind – and only differing in degree – as the productions of established writers; that many of the processes are shared too; and that the distance between the speaking voices of children and the nuances of printed works is not as great as some would suggest.

> Instead of there being a great gulf fixed between the mature and immature artist, their worlds lie very close together, their meanings are akin and the process by which they reach them is the same; the same process of dramatization is followed by both, the same poetic laws obeyed, and now we see that the same type of free phantasy is pursued. (p. 98)

Hourd's sensitivity to form is evident in her statements throughout the book, like this one (p. 103):

> Children are only likely to reach the mastery of form which the artist achieves when they are moving easily within their own experience . . . However, we have seen that it is one of the characteristics of child expression to anticipate later phases of development, so that it is important in the English lessons to provide these further reaches, although the resulting form may not be so satisfactory from adult standards. Let us make room, especially in adolescence, for all forms of expression at all levels of achievement.

Hourd almost strikes a balance between promotion of the voice in poetry and an awareness of form – but 'awareness' is about as far as it goes with regard to the formal features of poetry. As already suggested, the poems chosen to represent the range of poetic styles and, in a sense, to illustrate the thesis of the book, are formally conservative. The book, after all, is called *The Education of the Poetic Spirit*.

James Britton and the emergence of the poetic function

One of the central figures regarding the place of poetry and the nature of the poetic in this post-war period is James Britton, who published several articles in the fifties and sixties on poetry in schools (e.g. 1953, 1958, 1966 collected in *Prospect and Retrospect*, 1982). We will look at some of these early articles before discussing the poetic function and its influence upon contemporary thought in this area.

One of the early essays, 'Reading and Writing Poetry', sees the response of an eight-year-old boy to poems by James Stephens, de la Mare and Dickinson about cold weather as evidence of the directness of young children's relationships with the world (p. 9):

> It is part of the process of growing up to tone down our emotional responses by imposing an organized control upon them. We develop *habits* of response, and organize these habits into systems so that our long-term aims may not always be at the mercy of immediate emotional gratification . . . This is part of the price we pay

for becoming responsible members of society. Young children have no such responsibility and may enjoy the freedom of direct and vivid feeling.

This freshness of emotional response, unconstrained by adult propriety, is a direct result of the 'newness' of the poet's art. It is almost as if poetry operated in a pre-lapsarian world, reminding us, as adults, of the innocent vision and responses of childhood. The poet inhabits this world, and it is (ibid. p. 22):

> precisely because he retains a sense of the 'new-foundness', the freshness, and so the delight, of words that the poet is the kind of artist he is.

The consequence of this view of poetry is to see it as a kind of 'compensation' for the hardships of adult or adolescent life (ibid. pp. 9–10):

> We compensate ourselves, sometimes, by enjoying emotional experiences in a field in which there is no responsibility because no practical outcome is involved.

Despite the caveats and qualifications attached to this position, it remains one which is informed by the tradition of poetry running from Blake to Hughes; and, in turn, it has informed subsequent thinking and theorizing, both in Britton's own work and in practice in classrooms.

Let us explore this position further. Later in the 1958 essay, Britton defines 'poem' in these terms (p. 12):

> In the last analysis, a poem is a pattern, not of sounds or of movements, but of experience: it is *an* experience, a carefully organized, structured experience . . . It is a close-knit pattern: rhythm, rhyme and other sound effects, studied repetitions, cross-referring images, all combine to make it a seamless whole. It differs from prose in that it demands a special kind of attention – an awareness of the whole poem must accompany attention to each individual part.

Here is a crucial difference in emphasis, though not in kind, from the definitions offered earlier by the 11- and 12-year-olds from Ray Tarleton's classes. There, the definitions were more formal; here, it is *experience* that is the foundational element.

It seems true that a poem is a pattern of experience, and furthermore that it is an experience in itself. But the same could be said for a life, for the experiences of a day, for a novel: it is a statement at a level of generalization which will not help us define what is distinctive about a *poem*. We must also grant that poetry demands a special kind of attention. The texture of the pattern – its particular close-knit quality – is the most specific feature mentioned in this definition.

A further observation is the identification of poetry with the urge to express (ibid. p. 14):

> A poem . . . can be written only in response to some inner need in the writer, and if it comes off at all, it satisfies that need. Poetry arises, indeed, when something needs to be said and the need is satisfied by the mere saying. (This is not true only of poetry, of course: it applies also to the few choice words you may use when you drop a spanner on your toe!)

The contradiction in 'A poem . . . can be written only . . .' and 'This is not true only of poetry . . .' reveals the short-circuiting logic of this part of the argument. Not all poems need to be written in response to 'some inner need': occasional poems, for instance, don't fall into this category, and neither do functional public poems like *Absalom and Achitophel* or Tony Harrison's *The Blasphemer's Banquet*. The difference is that these poems, and others of their kind, are generated from a different poetic, from a different view of the place of poetry in society and therefore of the nature of the poem. If Dryden or Harrison did have an 'inner need', those needs are implicated and complicated by wider political needs. Their poems cannot be said to arise from the same need as a poem by Keats or the early Eliot (nor, indeed, can Eliot or Keats be assumed to attend the same muse).

Neither, for that matter, need poetry be associated with the imagination. The link has always been a strong one in the romantic tradition, but it is not an absolute one. Britton claims, in 'Words and the Imagination' (p. 21), that

> As far as words are concerned, it is in poetry above all that the penetrative and constructive powers of the imagination find expression. Poetry, says Professor Garrod, 'deals not with things as they are, but with things *as they matter*'.

First, there are poems in existence that are not informed or driven by the imagination any more than they are by other faculties; second, we need to look more closely at the claim that poetry deals with things as they *matter* rather than as they *are*.

The implication here, I think, is that because the imagination transforms 'things as they are' through the action of the poet's *interpretation* of experience, that the very act of selecting, transforming and fusing into some new combination (cf. Coleridge) gives the poem a moral dimension. Britton glosses the assertion thus (p. 21):

> The poet's interpretation of experience, since words have *meaning*, or represent concepts, is concrete, sensuous, emotional and *intellectual*. As a user of words the poet has a greater power to interpret experience since he exploits all the resources of words, while the prose writer uses only some of them. Poetry, for these reasons, will occupy a central position in the English teaching at most schools. It will be both written and read.

The distinction between poetry and prose is one to which we will return in detail in the next chapter, when those 'resources' are weighed one against the other.

When we turn to Britton's later work on the poetic, immediately we are faced with an extension and shift in focus. What was evident in the earlier work as an inclusiveness, a broad definition of the nature and effect of poetry, becomes distilled in the later work to the poetic *function* rather than its form.[1] In the appendix to *The Development of Writing Abilities, 11–16* (1975), the poetic is described as:

> A verbal construct, patterned verbalization of the writer's feeling and ideas. This category is not restricted to poems but would include such writings as a short story, a play, a shaped autobiographical episode.

That is to say, the poetic is closely allied to the aesthetic employment of words; it is not to be confused with 'poetry' or the 'poem', though these would almost certainly fall within this category. Nevertheless, the very term 'poetic' used here, and forming such a pillar of the theoretical construction that has come to be known as the Britton model, is predicated on an assumption about the nature of poetry.

The model drawn up by the Schools Council research team drew heavily on James Moffett's *Teaching the Universe of Discourse* (1968), but as Moffett admits in the foreword to the 1983 re-issue, poetry gets fairly short shrift in that seminal and influential book. On the spectrum of abstraction, from 'what is happening' (drama, reporting) through 'what happened' (narrative) to 'what happens' (exposition, the essay) and 'what might happen' (theorizing, argumentation), poetry runs along the whole range (pp. 46–7):

> It is interesting that poetry cannot be located by abstraction and person. To distinguish it from other discourses we have to invoke a different concept altogether – Suzanne Langer's division between discursive symbols and presentational symbols, a split which we may imagine running vertically down the abstractive spectrum. To the extent that it *does* differ, poetry is presentational symbolization, akin to music and art.

The sidelining of poetry is an evident weakness in the conception. Within the Moffett framework, one could say that the lyric operates in a seemingly mono-logic way alongside the dramatic in that it tries to capture the present; but its compressed argumentative power, its descriptive capacity and its ability to embrace and use narrative do indeed enable it to play the whole scale. Even *Active Voice* (1981) – one of Moffett's writing programmes based on the earlier theory – acknowledges that (p. 4):

> it was precisely the emphasis on logical development in the original version that caused me to slight poetry

but this slighting is not redressed by the appendix-like list of assignments for work in poetry at the end of the book.

So entangled are present conceptions of the poetic, poetry and the poem, that it is worth separating the strands and trying to see clearly how one model stands in relation to another; furthermore, it is important not to equate either Hourd's or Britton's position with that of 'creative writing', that amorphous and liberating 'movement' whose legacy we still see in the term 'creative' (as opposed to transactional or 'real world') use of language. (I include speech as well as writing here; why has 'creativity' been associated largely with writing and not with speech?) It has been all too easy to equate Britton's poetic function with the creative writing movement, but as is clear in the following paragraph, Britton is more than aware of the distinction (p. 31):

> During the middle sixties a strong movement towards creative writing developed in some English schools. It was assumed that, given some attractive stimulus, original,

profound and beautiful writing would emerge and teachers should do nothing to interfere with the 'free' expression of the creative imagination . . . But all worthwhile writing is creative in one way or another, and imagination is not confined to poetry. Nor is the writing of poems and stories free expression: here the writer is subject to constraints of many kinds, though he may have more options open to him than, say, a research student or a court reporter.

I will return to the creative writing movement later in this chapter. The important point to note here is that 'creative' can apply to 'all worthwhile writing', whether poetic or transactional.

Some exposition of Britton's poetic function is necessary for our argument to progress, such is the monumental nature of the conception. Poetic language uses language as an art medium; the words are selected to make 'an arrangement, a formal pattern' (p. 90). The pattern is made up of 'the phonic substance of language itself', 'the writer's feelings', 'events' (where there is narrative) and a 'pattern of ideas' which adds 'a characteristically poetic dimension to the writer's thinking'. In almost structuralist terms, it is added that (p. 90):

Consonance and dissonance between formal elements bind the writing into a complete whole, a single construct whether it be a sonnet or a novel, an epic or a curtain-raiser.

The language itself is the object of attention, 'by the writer and the reader, in a way that does not hold of non-poetic writing', and so in poetic writing 'language . . . exists for its own sake' (p. 91).

One of the most important points made by Britton with regard to poetic writing relates to the process of composing in this mode. My own small-scale study in the composing of narrative by 12- and 13-year-olds suggests that Britton's perception (p. 32) that detailed planning of poetic writing 'is not possible' is true, if overstated:

Once the conception has begun to emerge – what Langer calls the 'import' of the work – most children are ready to start writing. There will still be a place for insights, and illuminations that may alter and develop the work as it takes its shape, but these are much more likely to proceed as the writing proceeds. And they are so much the personal possession of the writer that the teacher has no place in their formation.

But it is interesting to compare this statement – developed more fully in 'Shaping at the Point of Utterance' (1982) – with the comments quoted earlier on the approaches used in creative writing classes in the mid-sixties, namely that 'It was assumed that, given some stimulus, original, profound and beautiful writing would emerge, and teachers *would do nothing to interfere with the "free" expression* of the creative imagination' (op. cit. p. 31).

Another important point is made in a more detailed account of the nature of poetic writing. Britton argues (p. 85) that the content of poetic writing, often more personal than that in transactional writing, will be made more accessible to an audience of strangers through the complex and subtle internal structure of the artefact: inner experience is, so to speak, given 'resonance' within the structure and the whole becomes *an experience of order*.

With these two points in mind, we can move on to take a closer look at the creative writing movement itself and what it signified for the writing and reading of poetry.

The creative writing movement

It is extraordinary the extent to which 'creative writing' was associated with poetry in this movement, and to a lesser extent with poetic prose. It was certainly the case that in the main, creative writing referred to writing in the poetic mould, despite Britton's disclaimer to the effect that all worthwhile writing could be termed 'creative'. A special edition of *English in Education* (the journal of the National Association for the Teaching of English) (Vol. 3, No. 3, Autumn 1969) will stand as an icon for this approach, even though it contains within it a variety of approaches.

In the editorial, the mapping is clear. Leslie Stratta refers to 'articles not only on "creative" writing, but also on "impersonal" or "referential" writing' (p. 3) and there follow several articles covering the stated range. Of those on creative writing, Raymond O'Malley's is perhaps the most illuminating. In 'Creative Writing in Schools', O'Malley accepts that 'one is not implying that other forms of writing are not also creative, but simply that, if what is creative is taken out of this particular kind of writing, there isn't much left' (p. 70). The strengths and gains made in this kind of writing are extolled by O'Malley as he refutes an assertion by Robert Conquest that much that goes for creative writing in schools is poetry in which 'children are encouraged to write down, regardless of rhythm, any reasonably emotional or intense set of phrases, provided this is divided up into the appearance of lines'. In a sense, the poem on which O'Malley bases his analysis does not matter here; what is at stake is the general set of qualities perceived to be valuable in this kind of writing. It includes the attempt to write in role and as oneself at the same time (and thus getting a double perspective on the subject and theme of the poem), emphasizing the balance and contrast of the felt experience in the semi-refrain; using line-division to emphasize key phrases; and giving overall shape and unity to the experience – 'all this within 120 words' (p. 72). It ought to be added that the poem in question was unrhymed, in two ten-line stanzas, the second set just to the right of the first. It did not therefore fall into any common stock of patterns from the literary tradition, nor on the other hand was it a free-form expression (if such a thing can be said to exist). In these and other ways, the poem seems testimony to the value of this approach to writing.

Interestingly, creative writing – and by implication, poetry – is seen not only as an antidote to the real world, but as an inoculation against it. Poetry – and by further implication, literary criticism – stands paramount in the fight against the forces of mass media and particularly the persuasive forms within the media, like advertising. It is part of the voice of the individual (but not of the people) fighting a rearguard action on humanitarian grounds; its weapons are the senses and reflection, the image and the expression of feelings. Typical of the poems generated by this approach are these opening lines from a poem by a year 10 girl, quoted by O'Malley, combining the record of the senses with a rather wistful memory of the whole experience:

It used to be fun, they say, remembering
A snatched night among the lights of the fair,
A swingboat ride, flying to the misty stars
She clinging to his jacket. Holding hands
Behind the candy floss stall, the sweet smell
Cloying their nostrils . . .

That particular poignancy and celebration of experience is representative of the best of the creative writing movement; the poem is poised, unrhymed, assured.

Robert Protherough, in an important article in *English in Education* (1978: p. 9) entitled appropriately 'When in doubt, write a poem', charts the demise of the creative writing movement while at the same time wanting to hold on to the best things about it:

Robert Witkin has pointed out that *creativity* as a term occurred little in psychological journals up to 1950, and thereafter rapidly increased in use, only to fade again a decade later. In the *British Education Index*, it does not appear in the titles of articles up to 1963 though it is foreshadowed by a few references to *free writing* and *free expression*. In 1964 there are three pieces explicitly on *creative writing*, by 1968–9 it has become a frequently used term, a popular topic; and then by 1973 it fades away again.

The emphasis on 'freedom' (one assumes not so much from formal strictures as from a pedagogical approach which 'gave titles' and which prescribed a narrow range of genres and set ways of achieving success in those genres) coupled with the centrality of the imagination are the hallmarks of this groundswell movement. At its best, there was a balance between such freedom of expression on the one hand, and the liberating formality of poetic structures on the other. It would be wrong to pitch structure against free expression here; despite experiments with relatively uncorseted writing in the fifties and sixties, the best work (as re-presented in anthologies like *The Excitement of Writing* (Clegg 1964) displayed all the qualities that the creative writing movement valued and promoted – freedom, imagination, vividness, originality, sensuousness and intensity – along with a certain degree of sensitivity to literary forms.

Whereas the examples of poems arrayed by Marjorie Hourd in *The Education of the Poetic Spirit* were formally conservative, there is sign of experimentation in *The Excitement of Writing*. About a third of the texts collected are poems, and these are almost exclusively in free verse form.

And as Summerfield and Summerfield point out in *Texts and Contexts* (1986), some structures liberate and others constrain. It would be premature to discard all notions of structure simply because the feeling was that structures *per se* were empty.

It seems clear now that the creative writing movement was pedagogical rather than formal in nature. It was a particular approach, concerning itself primarily with the process of writing rather than with the shape of the products; its aim was to stimulate and develop the imagination, nourish the sensibility and draw out expression from the children. Protherough sees this concern with process rather than product as one of the potential weaknesses of the model, along with a restriction of the kinds of writing practised, and the danger of badly chosen or presented stimuli. We can add to this the artificial polarity established and reinforced between 'creative' work on the one hand, and 'critical' and/or (by implication) 'non-creative' work on the other.

The reason for devoting several pages to the creative writing movement in a book on poetry should now be clear: poetry, because it happened to be the genre that conventionally embodied the ingredients of creative writing – imagination, sensuousness, vividness etc. – came to be almost synonymous with it. This influential but damaging alliance persists right up to the present.

Poetry and 'voice'

As Pam Gilbert (1989) points out, 'the predominant metaphor serving to hold together "authoring" and "the individual" in current writing pedagogy is the metaphor of "voice"' (p. 19) – and metaphor it indeed is, despite the founding of much contemporary theory about writing on what we know about *speech*. This is a complicated and intriguing area of debate, because while wanting to espouse a focus on text rather than voice, there is an element of the theory based on 'voice' that is important to retain, viz. the 'dialogic' nature of communication and the implied dialogic contexts of texts.

This apparent contradiction can be resolved by reference to the sources and manifestations of each of these positions. Those who champion the cause of 'voice' link it with the individual author, the expression of a single personality. Texts are assumed not to be 'lively' – sometimes not even to communicate – unless infused by 'voice', and from this viewpoint, 'text and author merge' (p. 19). Gilbert quotes Graves (1983):

> The writing process has a driving force called voice . . . it underlies every part of the process. To ignore voice is to present the process as a lifeless, mechanical act . . . Voice is the imprint of ourselves on our writing . . . Take the voice away and the writing collapses of its own weight.

The source of theories of the dialogic nature of spoken and written communication is largely Bakhtin (1981, 1986), and we will return to his viewpoint later in this section.

For the time being, let us pursue the notion of the connection between 'voice' and poetry. This connection is hinted at in the words of Elbow (1973: p. 6):

> In your natural way of producing words there is a sound, a texture, a *rhythm* – a voice – which is the main source of power in your writing.

That emphasis on rhythm (my italics), seems to point in the direction of poetry, and the connection is made explicit in much of the writing of the 'creative' school. As Gilbert suggests (p. 23):

> The poem is considered to be the vehicle of the emotions, a personal language form; and personal language is linked directly to the individual, to the expression of original ideas. The assumption underpinning such approaches to school poetry writing is that the construction of a poem is a relatively free task, as long as the author is emotionally inspired.

This attitude towards poetry – one which identifies the poem with the writer of the poem – can leave teachers in a difficult position regarding the response to such writing. Is poetry to be 'marked' in the same way as other writing? Can it be 'assessed' for a coursework folder? Is the freedom to be found in poetry writing licentious, or does it involve responsibilities with regard to form? Gilbert points to disparities between the socially constructed worlds of the poem in school and in the wider reading public.

From another angle, David Jackson (1986), in 'Poetry and the speaking voice', sets up such a polarity between oral directness and the 'academic/introspective/scholarly poem tradition' in order to argue the case for the presence of the speaking voice in poetry. It is an important case. In broad terms, all English teachers would probably want their students to 'give voice' to their feelings and thoughts. 'Voice', as well as its precise literal meaning, connotes 'self'. Like a finger print, the individual voice reveals identity and it comes to represent the concept of individuality. Furthermore, 'voice' is associated with a right or privilege – a right of an individual to speak *on behalf of a group* in an assembly – and more generally still, with the expression of opinion, with democracy and with the will of the people, as Paolo Freire suggests when he says,

> As an event calling forth the critical reflection of both the learners and the educators, the literary process must relate *speaking* the word to *transforming reality*, and to man's role in this transformation. Such a perception will lead the learners to recognize a much greater right than that of being literate. They will ultimately realize that, as men, they have the right to have a voice.

Much conspires against such expressiveness, and it is right that English teachers have fought to preserve that space in the curriculum. Three points must be made clear at this point, however: one is that poetry is not entirely synonymous with 'voice', the second is that notions of expression and empowerment are weakened if 'form' is excluded from the equation and thirdly, 'form', 'shape' and 'genre' are as much a feature of speech as they are of writing. These three points are part of the reason why too close an alliance between poetry and voice *in opposition to* the literary (written) tradition is dangerous.

The first point is evident if we look outside the narrow tradition of late romantic expressive poetry. Not all poems are infused with a particular voice, nor for that matter are they all 'expressive' in the sense of emanating from the 'self'. The self and its voices are much more varied and complex than this formulation suggests: modulations of tone, shifts in rhythmic patterning and adjustments of form and style for different audiences are all aspects of this variety. Poetry cannot be limited to 'feelings' or some deep elusive single self.

That first point is of relevance to the kind of poetry read and written in schools, and the overall view of poetry that obtains within a school. The second point is a more specific one. There is a point between the urge to express and the existing gamut of literary forms at which interaction between the two is vital for both: existing literary (written and spoken) forms can offer scaffolding for the emergent 'voice' to find shape; at the same time, the scaffolds are reshaped by the urgency of the expression. To deny children the experience of published poetry in order to give them free rein as far as their own expression goes is to condemn them to reinventing the wheel. Many of the existing literary forms will increase their capacity to express, if introduced judiciously.

The third point follows on from the second: it is naive to think that speech does not take shape, and that writing does – just because we can 'see' it on the page. Speech, as Bakhtin (1986) makes clear, is as determined by social shaping as much as writing is. 'Form', though it might originate in the visual arts, is applicable to sound as well as to print. So there is no 'pure expressivity' to place in opposition to sophisticated literary form.

Form – the shape utterances take, 'compositional structure' – is the key, and as has already been evidenced in the previous chapter, Ray Tarleton's first years showed admirable awareness of it with regard to poetry. Form is not abstract and 'empty', but is grounded in the range of examples of speech and poetry that we encounter. It is a feature common to literature and all forms of language, which is why it is interesting to put poems alongside newspaper reports (see Culler 1975), advertisements, travel brochures, and prose in general as well as alongside speech genres (conversation, debate, speech, argument, story etc.). Such practice teaches us about language at the same time as sharpening our awareness of the differences between the various forms and their applications. It is not so much a question of 'poetic conventions' at the level of the word or sentence (corresponding to phonetic, lexical and syntactic linguistics) – the level of form which critics of this position often assume is the level of interest – but form at the level of the text.

This means that we can begin to look at poetry, not as a form on some kind of pedestal or as a distinct and separate mode of discourse from the rest of communication, but as a genre among other genres. That is to say, rather than approach it by trying to define its effect, we are now in a position to look at its nature at the level of the text. And because texts of any kind (in both speech and writing) are constituted socially, we must take that dimension into account.

As Bakhtin's translators put it, poems are:

secondary (complex) utterances [and a] one-sided orientation towards primary
genres inevitably leads to a vulgarization of the entire problem

of speech genres (1986: p. 62). Bakhtin is interesting on the poem, though much
of his energy is focused on the novel. In *The Dialogic Imagination* (1981: p. 298),
he briefly addresses the question of rhythm in poetry:

> Rhythm, by creating an unmediated involvement between every aspect of the
> accentual system of the whole . . . destroys in embryo those social worlds of speech
> and of persons that are potentially embedded in the word . . . As a result . . . a
> tension-filled unity of language is achieved in the poetic work.

What Bakhtin doesn't mention is that rhythm is a feature of speech too (see
Leech 1969), so that the tension 'achieved in the poetic work' is precisely the
tension generated between the looser (or less consciously crafted) rhythms of
speech and the usually tighter rhythms of poetry and music. Bakhtin is also
critical of the over-emphasis of the expressive function. In ironic tone, he
declares (1986: p. 67):

> Language arises from man's need to express himself, to objectify himself. The
> essence of any form of language is somehow reduced to the spiritual creativity of the
> individuum.

And later he adds (p. 80),

> The better our command of genres, the more freely we employ them, the more fully
> and clearly we reveal our own individuality in them (where this is possible and
> necessary), the more flexibly and precisely we reflect the unrepeatable situation of
> communication . . .

Don Gutteridge and 'naive poetry'

It is partly in opposition to the notion of a single, discoverable 'voice' in
children-as-writers that Gutteridge's book, *The Dimension of Delight* (1988) takes
its stand. In particular, it is at pains to dissociate itself from the alliance between
the expressive function in Britton's formulation, 'voice' in its univocal sense, and
poetry. Gutteridge notes at the beginning of the book how he withdrew in
confidence during the early eighties in the light of the 'process movement' in
writing (pp. xiv–xv):

> Now suddenly the very idea of *shaped writing* as an intrinsically valuable, psychologi-
> cally embedded, developmental form of human expression was being seriously
> questioned.

He makes a close connection between the writing-process approaches – exemplified by the work of Graves (1983) and Calkins (1986) – and 'expressive/
personal-narrative formats' (p. 3), though it should be pointed out that his fusion
of the Britton model with that of the writing-process movement is questionable.
But not only did the idea of shaped writing wither in the face of the process

approach; Gutteridge sees the creative writing movement collapsing 'under the twin pressures of the Transactional and the Expressive' (p. 14) too. The general effect of this emphasis on the expressive and transactional, seen (rightly in my opinion) as the stronger side of the Brittonian model along with the hybrid offshoot, 'process writing', was to diminish the poetic function.

It is the expressive function (though he calls it 'mode', which complicates if not entirely negating his argument) that Gutteridge reserves much of his criticism for, and he draws on Frye (1963: p. 19) to support him:

> Frye's schema differs [from Britton's] in two radical respects ... He would not accept the use of the term Poetic to cover both sophisticated Verse and Prose rhythms, and he would not accept Britton's major developmental hypothesis: that the Expressive mode – tied to speech, familiar audience and to the ego expressing *itself* – is *the* primary mode, the universal matrix which all other forms of writing evolve out of or are informed by. In each case, his reason would be the same: there is a third Primary Rhythm, one that is coeval with the Expressive/Associative impulse and is unique in its nature and functioning: Verse.

Frye's interest is primarily generic (1963: pp. 25–6):

> ... verse is closely related to dance and song [cf. Hughes' definitions in Chapter 2]: it is closely related to the child's own speech, which is full of chanting and singing, as well as of primitive verse forms like the war cry and the taunt song (1963: pp. 25–6)

but it is not a rigid, purely taxonomic definition of verse. It seeks to explore the evolution of the genre both historically and ontologically; it is thus as developmental a hypothesis as Britton's, the difference being this tantalizingly difficult distinction between 'function' (Britton's line) and 'mode' or 'genre' (Frye's). However, we can make some tentative generalizations which will help us to see this difference in approach more clearly.

The functional approach is expressed adjectivally ('poetic', 'expressive', 'transactional') whereas the modal approach is usually characterized by nouns ('mode', 'form', 'genre'). The functional is concerned with effects and intentions; it is closer to speech-act theory; the actual language produced, whether it be speech or writing, is seen as a means to some end, and the approach attempts to define and categorize those ends. Strictly speaking, then, this approach does not have its principal focus on language *per se*, but rather on the actions of language. The modal approach, on the other hand, is more concerned with texts and utterances as entities. The functions of the text or utterance are less surely defined (partly because they aren't as evident as the text itself) and the focus is on the factors which bear upon the text *as evidenced in the text*. These may be concerned with authorial intention, with historical context, with the social construction of the text and/or with the reader's response, but they will always 'come back to' the text or utterance.

We can probably see now that each of these approaches has a different legacy. The functional approach owes much of its character to psychological research and tenets. Britton's mentors, as it were, are Freud and Piaget, Harding and subsequently Vygotsky. The modal approach owes its shape to literary criticism (Frye's principal *mode d'emploi*), but a longer tradition on which it draws is that of rhetoric. To summarize the difference rather crudely, the functional approach is more concerned with process and the child, and the modal approach is more concerned with the product: the text or utterance.

Part of the aim of the present book is to forge a new synthesis from the 'thesis' represented by the Hourd-Britton-creative writing line, and its 'antithesis' in the formalist tradition. If the argument of this book seems to favour the latter, it is simply to redress the balance between the two viewpoints. There will also have to be considered the sociological viewpoint, which would see such a synthesis as a union of the two weaker positions in a triangle of which it has the ascendant position.

But before we leave the distinction between function and mode, it is important for the purposes of the argument to break down the various divisions of 'mode' so that we can use them as working terms in later chapters with confidence and clarity. *Mode* can be defined as the broadest of the three terms, 'mode', 'genre' and 'form'. It is, as the term suggests, a way of organizing discourse. Examples would be narrative, argument or poetry. At the generic level, these break down into types like the novel, the short story; essays; and lyric or epic poetry. Yet further, at the level of *form*, we have sub-types like detective novel, sonnet, haiku etc.

Let us return now to the point that Frye makes, and which Gutteridge uses to reinforce his argument that the expressive is not as univocal as Britton seems to suggest. Frye (1963: p. 26) asserts that it is verse rhythm which informs much of the written/spoken literature of the child's schooling and his or her culture:

> But poetry, the main body of which is verse [see distinction discussed in Chapter 2] is always the central powerhouse of a literary education. It contributes, first, the sense of rhythmical energy ... It contributes, too, as the obverse of this, the sense of leisure, of expert timing of the swing and fall of cadences. Then there is the sense of wit and heightened intelligence, resulting from seeing disciplined words marching along in metrical patterns and in their inevitably right order. And there is a sense of concreteness that we can get only from the poet's use of metaphor and visualized imagery. Literary education of this kind, its rhythm and leisure slowly soaking into the body and its wit and concreteness into the mind, can do something to develop a speaking and writing prose style that comes out of the depths of personality and is a genuine expression of it.

It will be immediately recognized that what Frye is saying about poetry is not that different from what Hourd, Britton or the creative movement were saying: the emphasis on the centrality of poetry in a literary education, the sense of wit (Hourd's cognitive dimension) and heightened intelligence, the pleasures to be gained from the sense of order (despite Frye's militaristic image!); and, in particular, the sense of concreteness and the expressivity of poetry. But there are differences too. Frye's 'sense of rhythmical energy' as *primus inter pares* is significantly more emphatic than in any of the other justifications for poetry.

There are two points in the Frye argument that I have taken up elsewhere in the book. The first is the distinction between verse and poetry, and the second – the more important one for our purposes – is the distinction between the rhythmic energies of poetry and its leisure-inducing cadences. This latter subject will be discussed fully in the following chapter.

To summarize the points that Gutteridge is making: first, the development of an appreciation of and an ability to compose verse rhythms is not a late feature in children's growth; second, it is there from the start, and informs the consciousness as much as the expressive; third, and as a result of the first two points, it is wrong to assume that there is a single 'expressive' matrix from which the diversification of literary and linguistic modes and functions emerges (p. 22):

> Frye's schema suggests that the Associative and Verse Rhythms are *equally* primary. Hence one could not logically be the matrix for the other . . .

Poetry is not a separate language

In the opening chapter of *Towards A Speech-Act Theory of Literary Discourse* (1977), Mary Louise Pratt demolishes the arguments associated primarily with the Prague School, but pervasive throughout our century, of the distinction between 'poetic' and 'everyday' or 'prosaic' language. The term 'poetic', of course, refers not only to poetry but also to all literary forms and genres; and further still, to all aesthetic forms. However, in keeping with the subject of this book, we will confine ourselves to the application of this argument to poetry and poems.

The chapter is called 'The "Poetic Language" Fallacy', and follows an introduction in which the Prague School's claims are laid out. One of the central claims is that 'poetic language must be studied in and of itself'. According to Pratt (p. xvi)

> [this] amounts to a restatement of the art for art's sake credo of the avant-garde. For the past century at least, the belief that literature is intrinsically distinct from and opposed to all the other things we do with language has had at its heart the belief that literature is intrinsically superior to them, a belief which is still accepted in many critical quarters today. And this belief generally comes accompanied by a number of others.

These include a distinction between poetical and practical experience, between a poetic and practical universe, and between the poet and the 'practical man'. From this point of view, it is the internal coherence of the poetical work which counts, almost to the exclusion of meaning and communication. Poems are seen as formal constructs, composed of repetition of phoneme groups, rhythm, melody and other musical features; images, metaphors and so on – all, in a sense, reflecting in upon themselves in some hermetically sealed form of discourse. In comparison, the language of the world is 'a medium essentially practical, perpetually changing, soiled, a maid of all work' (Valéry 1938: p. 81).

Not only is poetic language superior to the language of the world, it is also timeless. Pratt quotes Mallarmé (1886–95: p. 43):

> Language, in the hands of the mob, leads to the same facility and directness as does money; but in the Poet's hands, it is turned above all, into dream and song; and, by the constituent virtue and necessity of an art which lives in fiction, it achieves its full efficacy.

The suggestion made by Pratt that the notion of the supremacy of literary (including poetic) language has hardly been questioned is both startling and not quite true. There has been a recurrent, though not always successful, attempt to rediscover the rhythms and intonations of living speech in poetry and in the novel: Hemingway, Raymond Carver, Pinter, Eliot, Yeats and William Carlos Williams all come to mind in their different ways. And there has been a persistent, and again not wholly influential, line of Marxist and sociological criticism which we will discuss shortly. But the general outline remains as Pratt describes it. In our own tentative hypothesis that rhythm plays a more prominent part in the definition of poetry than has been acknowledged to date, how can we answer the implied criticism of this sociological viewpoint?

First, it has to be agreed – and indeed strengthens the argument – that the split between poetic and everyday language is overstated, if not fallacious. If poetry has no bearing on the language of everyday speech, its life-blood is cut off and it will wither and die. The formulation of the poetic as opposed to the transactional seems to reflect this split – even though the polarity is disguised as a continuum.

Second, it has to be admitted that rhythm exists in 'everyday' speech as well as in poetry. The difference is that in poetry the rhythm is consciously employed. Pratt seems to miss or skirt round this fundamental point. Perhaps we should address this question here, because the centrality of rhythm to poetry is an important plank in the stage this book is trying to build.

Pratt quotes Brik (1927) who makes a distinction between syntax and rhythm and who suggests that the very tension between these in a text constitutes 'the peculiarity of poetry' (p. 122). She then assumes that Brik sees 'rhythm' as literary and syntax as part of everyday discourse, but that clearly isn't Brik's claim; all he says is that rhythms 'complicate' syntax. But (Pratt 1977: p. 13):

> hence, according to Brik, one can 'translate' an utterance from poetic to nonpoetic language by wiping out its rhythmic organization: 'By rearranging words we can deprive a line of poetry of its poetic shape and turn it into a phrase from the sphere of ordinary speech'

Pratt suggests that Brik's comparison is 'illegitimate' because linguists who deal in syntax never posed the question of rhythmic organization. I suggest two solutions to this impasse: one is that Brik meant 'conscious rhythm', as I have formulated it above; the other is that the real problem with Brik's comparison is that it is between poetry and *speech* when what he means is a distinction between poetry and *prose*. It is true that when you de-line a poem, you lose its poetic nature; it is no longer a poem. It has become prose.

Third, in speech-act theory and from the sociological standpoint, discourse tends to be predicated upon *speech*. But despite the health of poetry being dependent upon the living, interactive, contextual nature of speech, most of us *write* and *read* it; that is to say, it is primarily print-oriented, and the contexts of the printed word are broader and less easily defined than those of the spoken word. So when Pratt presents as 'negative proof' of the indistinguishability of literary and non-literary material the 'fact' that texts cannot always be identified as literature on sight (p. 6), her proof cannot hold for poetry, where in most cases the text can *literally* be identified as poetry on sight.

Another important assumption that we should question is one mentioned by Pratt later in her chapter, in regard to the work of Stankiewicz (1961). This is the assumption that the most 'poetic' of poetic kinds of language is that of the lyric. The lyric is seen as the ' "marked" pole' of a continuum from non-poetic to poetic language, the most extreme and purest kind of self-referential language. The language used to describe this assumption is revealing: the shift in emphasis from external information to the message itself is a 'transformation of the non-poetic linear sequence into a poetic pluridimensional sequence' (Pratt 1977: p. 28). This metamorphic transformation is akin to the metaphorical dimension that is supposed to be the province of poetry, but what is also interesting is the notion that the overall transformation is one from a 'linear' (narrative?) sequence to a 'pluridimensional' (multi-layered, metaphorical) sequence. Again, this distinction is not true even of lyric poetry (which sometimes takes linear, narrative form, e.g. some of the poems of Carver or Brecht), let alone the whole of poetry. The primacy of the lyric will be discussed further in Chapter 5.

I suggested earlier that a synthesis was possible between the two seemingly opposed views of the 'growth' theorists – those who see poetry as one of the central movers in the education of the imagination and the spirit – and the formalists, who would wish to separate the language of poetry from that of the everyday world. However, such a synthesis would not be a viable one in the eyes of sociological theorists because both approaches tend to exclusiveness: the first focusing on the growth of the individual sensibility and the second on the text. Without a consideration of the social contexts within which the poem operates, they believe that there can be no satisfactory picture of the nature of poetry and of the way it functions.

This sociological viewpoint is given expression in an essay by Voloshinov entitled 'Discourse in Life and Discourse in Poetry: Questions of Sociological Poetics' (1926, reprinted in Shukman, A. (Voloshinov 1983), *Bakhtin School Papers*). The basic premise informing the rest of the essay is that 'The aesthetic . . . is only a variety of the social' (1983: p. 7), and so (p. 9):

those methods which ignore the social essence of art and attempt to find its nature and peculiarities only in the organization of the work-thing [text], are in fact constrained to *project* the social interaction of the creator and perceiver on to various aspects of the material and the devices which give it form.

This is not the occasion on which to explore the rest of this argument further; it is sufficient for now to focus on two aspects of the argument which bear directly on the preoccupations of this book. These are the question of intonation and the nature and function of rhythm in a poem.

One of the most fascinating points in the essay is that intonation is seen to be the bridging element between 'discourse and the non-verbal context' (p. 13); it always operates 'on the border' (p. 14). It must be remembered that Voloshinov is talking about speech here, and not about writing. He gives an exposition of how the single word 'Well' could act as the basis for a number of different interpretations, *dependant upon context*. The key linguistic feature that helps in defining that context is intonation (p. 16):

Intonation in real-life speech is in general far more metaphorical than words, the ancient mythopoeic still as it were lives on in it. Intonation sounds as though the world around the speaker were still full of animate forces ... while the ordinary metaphors of conversational language have in the main become effaced, and semantically words have become paltry and prosaic.

It is interesting to reflect upon the fact that many twentieth-century poets have flattened intonation in their readings. Recordings of Eliot, Yeats, Pound, Larkin and others – poets who consciously incorporate speech into their work – are cases in point. For them, intonation is less important than rhythm, and the former is reduced to highlight the latter. Furthermore, it is more difficult to 'read' intonation off the page – to convert print into speech – than it is to read the rhythm of a poem: the very arrangement of the lines, the play of metre against speech rhythms, suggest ways in which the poem can be performed. I suggest that rhythm is one of the ways in which 'the poetic work is a powerful condenser of non-spoken social evaluations' (ibid. p. 19) – at least as important, if not more so, than intonation.

Rhythm and metaphor – the subjects of the next chapter – are accounted for thus by the sociological approach (p. 20):

The ideological evaluation expressed by form need not become part of the content in the shape of a moral, political or other maxim. The evaluation remains in the rhythm, in the actual *evaluational impulse* of the epithet, or metaphor, in the manner in which the depicted event is *unfolded*.

Summary

This chapter began with a look at the pioneering work of Marjorie Hourd, and then traced the development of James Britton's notion of the poetic. These influential writers were seen to have a connection with the creative writing movement, in which poetry gained ascendancy, but reservations were made about some aspects of the application of their theories, and distinctions made between their various positions. However, both writers can be seen to be part of a late Romantic flowering in poetic theory: their view of the centrality of the imagination, of concrete experience, of the deployment of the senses in the writing of poetry stands as testament to the romantic tradition.

Notions of the poetic from these points of view stand in opposition to 'everyday' language, and in this sense, the group of writers just mentioned have something in common with a pervasive twentieth century attitude which sees poetic language as something different from and separate from the language of transactions in the world. This attitude finds expression in the work of the Prague School and in the subsequent work of many linguists working in the field of poetics; their focus is primarily on the text itself, rather than on the functions of the text or the supposed effects it has on children's imaginations and sensibilities. In practical terms, this point of view has much in common with literary criticism (especially practical criticism) and finds further expression in the work of writers like Frye and Gutteridge, who see form as central to the argument.

But this view in itself is criticized by the sociological standpoint, which sees neither of the two positions already mentioned as having the scope to account for poetry (or any other form of discourse, for that matter). It sees a synthesis between them as inadequate without the sociological and contextual dimension to poetry being taken into account.

It is to the formal nature of poetry that we turn in the next chapter, and to the wider sociological context in Chapter 5. Only then can we move on to practical considerations about the reading and writing of poetry in schools – hopefully more fully informed about what we are trying to do, and how we might tackle the problem with poetry.

Note

1 In this respect I think the work of Britton and the London Writing Group has been open to misrepresentation. The conception of the 'poetic' is functional, and should not be conflated with poetic *form* in the narrower sense with which I am concerned in this book. My aim in this section is to make this distinction clear.

4 Rhythm

Repetition is the fundamental phenomenon of poetic form.

Barbara Herrnstein Smith in *Poetic Closure*

Each of the chapters in this book so far has referred to *rhythm* as being an important feature of poetry, if not *the* distinguishing feature of the genre. We have had Ted Hughes' part-definition of poetry as a 'dance in words', the definitions by Ray Tarleton's 11 to 12-year-olds ('a sort of rhythmic story', 'thought displayed in rhythmic pattern'), and Stankiewicz's suggestion that line arrangement – and hence rhythm – is the distinguishing feature of poetry as opposed to prose. Is rhythm the key distinguishing feature of poetry? If rhythm is also a feature of speech and prose, what kind of rhythm might be particular to poetry? How do we describe and evaluate the effect of rhythm in a poem? Is poetry really distinguishable from prose? And if we can gain some perspective on the role of rhythm in poetry, might some of the problem with poetry be solved? Let us now examine these claims and questions in more detail.

Poetry and prose

It seems in retrospect that it was in the interests of the creative writing movement *not* to draw too close a distinction between poetry and prose. Too much attention to the form of the writing would have distracted both writer and reader from the imaginative and recreative energies of this approach. And, in many ways, what was being written for the most part was either poetry or poetic prose. James Britton, in his 1958 article, suggests that (op. cit. p. 13):

> If we refrain from drawing too close a distinction between what is poetry and what is prose . . . we shall find a good deal of poetry is being written in school.

However, a distinction between poetry and prose can help us, at least, to see poetry more clearly for what it is, despite Auden's assertion that 'it is a sheer waste of time to look for a definition of the difference between poetry and prose' (1975: p. 23). We will know that if we take a particular route in the process of writing something, that certain constraints and possibilities are brought to bear on our writing. The constraints are not inhibiting; on the contrary, the distinctive structures, laws, patterns and shapes of particular forms and genres can act as supports and scaffolds for us to build our work. Or, to look at it another way, and to change the metaphor to something more organic, the *shape* of a particular piece of writing can emerge gradually, and reflect the content and purpose of its message, but nevertheless will still be some kind of shape. The argument that writing can be innocent of form is plainly naive. Even the most radical of breakaways from conventional forms creates a new form; it needn't be defined in relation to the original form from which it broke away, but its new form can be described in formal terms. And to counter Auden, we can say that complex though the relationship between poetry and prose is, it is worth exploring if only to clarify what we mean by poetry. Without that clarification, we can hardly justify its presence in a curriculum.

Prose, in general, 'goes right up the edge of the page'. The 'page' is the page of a printed book or of the sheet of paper on which you are writing. Now the printed page only takes the shape it does because of i) the nature of books and ii) various decisions that have been made by the designer and printer of the book as to how many words there will be on each page (itself a consequence of size and nature of typeface, size of page and economies that determine those decisions). If novels, for instance (most of which are written in prose – but not all!), were not squeezed into books, but could float freely and find their own shape, one sentence would follow another and they would probably extend in a long linear string from point A to point B – often several miles away. Indeed, with novels like *War and Peace* or *Gravity's Rainbow*, you are beginning to extend around the planet or towards the moon.

Of course, it is not quite as singular a line as that. Most novels (but again, not all) are divided into parts or chapters or sections. Those large divisions are in turn usually divided into paragraphs; and those paragraphs into sentences. But these sub-divisions are indicative of time-breaks or topic-breaks or all the other reasons for starting new sentences, paragraphs and chapters. They do not radically affect the *linear* momentum of prose, the quality that takes it beyond the edge of the page. To put it another way, the form a novel takes within a book is imposed from without, by the limitations of the book. A chapter may begin on the same page as the end of the previous chapter, or it may begin on a new page: it doesn't matter as far as the shape of the novel goes.

Here we come on to a crucial distinction – one indicated but not fully developed by Stankiewicz (1961). Even a novel or short story with pronounced rhythmical qualities – like *The Rainbow*, *Ulysses* or any such work incorporating a refrain – or, for that matter, any prose that is richly imagistic, like a lot of the material generated by the creative writing movement or some of Dylan Thomas' work – cannot be defined as poetry. They might be 'poetic' in the broader sense of that word, and they might even acquire the tag 'poetic prose', but they are not poems.

This distinction is crucial because without it, we are subject to all the confusion and misunderstanding of the nature of poetry that is one of its 'problems'. How, then, does poetry stand in relation to prose?

For a start, poems do not go 'right up to the edge of the page'. A look at most poems will immediately confirm this obvious but important characteristic. The function of this visual fact is partly to determine the way the text should be read, and seeing that such an imprint is to do with the poem's arrangement *in time*, and in particular with the relationship of one line to another in the poem, it is principally a rhythmic marker. In English, the tonal nature of the poem is more difficult to mark in print, and the tempo is an overall extra-textual feature that is rarely, if ever, indicated by the words on the page – even though it is a distinctive feature of any performance of the poem.

We can thus say that rhythm is a distinctive formal feature of poetry. It is there in prose in the grand sweep of a section, chapter or in the work as a whole; but it is only in poetry that its takes prominence as a consciously formal feature of the line and stanza. This is a rather fine distinction, it might be argued. Is it not true of prose, as well as of poetry, that the text takes place in time and that there is rhythmical relationship set up in the tension between the overall work and its various sections and sub-sections? Yes, it is true. Is it not also true that a piece of prose may be 'translated' into poetry by the simple rearrangement of the text into individual 'lines'? Yes, that is also true; but it is also the key to the difference between the two modes of representation.

It is at this point in the argument that we can return to Frye (1963). In *The Well-Tempered Critic*, he examines the distinctions between verse and prose in terms of the rhythmic units that constitute typical examples of the two discourses. Of the three main kinds of discourse that he defines, speech is characterized by associative rhythm, prose by syntactic rhythm (with the unit of discourse being the sentence) and verse by regularly repeated accent or metre. These are the 'three primary rhythms of verbal expression' (p. 24) and all three are involved in writing, 'but one is normally the dominating or organizing rhythm' (p. 25).

It is immediately apparent that this formulation is both helpful and arguable. One of its strengths is that it breaks down the opposition between poetry and prose which sees prose as somehow related to 'ordinary speech'. We can see now that this formula is the result of a false syllogism (based on false premises) which says that poetry is highly wrought language, that prose is different from poetry and therefore that prose is like speech. Another strength comes from its focus on rhythm as the distinguishing feature of the different kinds of discourse; this focus has a historical dimension, suggesting that the rhythms of verse pre-date the development of prose rhythms, both in cultural and literary (and pre-literary) history and in the language development of the child.

On the other hand, the free verse rhythm has a secondary position in this model, defined in relation to the primary verse rhythm. The early assertion that 'No free verse, such as Whitman's, is verse in my sense, however important as poetry' (p. 24) is qualified later (pp. 55–6) with:

The associative rhythm belongs, in its pure form, to undeveloped ordinary speech or
to the representing of such speech in fiction or drama; but in conventionalized form,
it can also become a third type of literary rhythm.

But even this is not free verse rhythm. That belongs to one of the secondary
'discontinuous' combinations of the primary rhythms: verse rhythm 'influenced'
by associative rhythm perhaps – or vice-versa. The inability of Frye's model to
account for free verse is a result of its basis in the three modes of discourse: free
verse, we know, can approximate music or prose rhythm as well as it approximates
speech. Rather than look at the particular rhythms generated by free verse, he has
chosen first to outlaw it from verse altogether, then to bring it back into the fold as
a secondary version of his definition of verse. The insensitivity to additive rhythm
as opposed to the regular repetitive rhythms we call metres causes this blind-spot.
Perhaps there should be *four* primary rhythms? And another of Frye's distinctions
– between hieratic and demotic style within poems – seems even less of an issue
now that it was in the 60s. Most contemporary poets have embraced the demotic
with an energy that causes us little problem as we adjust to the diction of the
poem.

Before looking at some texts to test the validity of these distinctions, a brief
summary of the position might be useful. What is being suggested here is that it is
worth making a distinction between poetry and prose, not only because we need a
firm basis on which to build a justification for the writing and study of poetry, but
also (and more fundamentally) because the nature of poetic texts has often been
clouded in mystique. Comparing poetic form with prose is one way of trying to
see the nature of poetry more clearly (though it could be argued that by
comparing poetry to *prose* we are highlighting certain features of poetry at the
expense of others).

Prose, it has been argued, is text that is not concerned with rhythmic shape of
its statements. There are larger-scale rhythms at play, particularly in prose
narrative where the relationship between supposed 'objective' linear time in the
world and the time structure of the novel or story is a characteristic phenomenon
(see Genette 1980, 1988; Ricoeur 1984, 1985, 1988), but the rhythms of the line
and stanza or section in relation to the work as a whole is not the focus of
attention. It is as if, with poetry, we are using a microscope to get up close to the
language. At this distance, rhythm seems to be operating at every level of the
discourse, and our attention to this feature of poetic writing has been heightened
by the presence of free verse, with its rhythmical unit being the line rather than
the 'foot'.

Let us look at a few examples of texts which challenge or test the bounds of
these distinctions between prose and poetry.

Here is a 'line' of poetry from Walt Whitman's 'Carol of Occupations':

Iron-works, forge-fires in the mountains, or by the river-banks – men around feeling
the melt with huge crowbars – lumps of ore, the due combining of ore, limestone,
coal – the blast-furnace and the puddling-furnace, the loup-lump at the bottom of

the melt at last – the rolling-mill, the stumpy bars of pig-iron, the strong, clean-
shaped T-rail for railroads;

It doesn't matter where the breaks along the line take place (in fact they are
different as printed here from the text they are taken from), and it doesn't matter
whether the right-hand margin is justified or not. Usually, features to do with
arrangements like this matter a great deal to poetry, but here they do not. The
reason is, of course, that the line of poetry begins at 'Iron-works' and ends at
'railroads'. Crucial to our argument, however, is that 'railroads' does mark the
end of the line, and as such is the end of the rhythmical unit of the poem. It could
have been marked with a full-stop, a comma or with no punctuation at all – these
do not affect the fact that it is the end of a line of poetry.

It looks more like a line of poetry when we set it in its immediate context. It is
flanked by these lines:

Coal-miners, and all that is down there, – the lamps in the darkness, echoes, songs,
   what meditations, what vast native thoughts looking through smutch'd faces,
Iron-works, forge-fires in the mountains, or by the river-banks – men around
   feeling the melt with huge crowbars – lumps of ore, the due combining of ore,
   limestone, coal – the blast-furnace and the puddling-furnace, the loup-lump at
   the bottom of the melt at last – the rolling-mill, the stumpy bars of pig-iron, the
   strong, clean-shaped T-rail for railroads;
Oil-works, silk-works, white-lead-works, the sugar-house, steam-saws, the great
   mills and factories;

and then by several more such lines in the sixth section of a poem of seven
sections. At the other end of the spectrum, lines consisting of single words, like

spring

from e.e. cummings' 'In Just-/spring . . .' or even parts of words, like his

rr

from 'carry' in 'o to be in finland . . .' still stand as lines. Perhaps, in the light of
these examples, we can refine our definition further to say that the distinctive
feature of poetry is that rhythm operates as a formally identifying feature at every
level of language, from the whole text, down through its sections and stanzas to its
individual lines, words and sounds or lexical units. It is as if the 'normal' linguistic
hierarchy has been slightly dislocated to place the 'line', rather than the sentence,
at the crucially pivotal point in the discourse; or that the rhythm of the poem, as
signalled in the line, runs across the whole message.

Prose poems are a form that would seem to directly challenge this part-
definition of poetry, and indeed the challenge is difficult to resist. Although they
are quite rare (how many writers can you think of that use the form?), they are still
generically poems. Some of the best contemporary prose poems have been
written by Solzhenitsyn and are collected in his volume *Stories and Prose Poems*
(1973): they range between about 100 and 400 words in length, lack the narrative

structure of stories, and are intensely 'poetic' and resonant. The borderline between these 'poems' and short shorts or 'sudden' fiction (i.e. fiction ranging from under 100 words up to about 2,000 words in length) is hard to define. Life would be easier for the cataloguer if these prose poems were classified as 'poetic short prose' or something to that effect, because that is what they are. They seem to be called 'poems', not because of their structural and formal qualities, but almost by default. Prose won't have them because the bastion of prose fiction is the novel: short stories themselves struggle for recognition, let alone 'short shorts' or prose poems. The *poetic* qualities these prose poems have are compression, lyricism and the use of imagery to resonate and suggest meaning.

The same is true of Baudelaire's prose poems. Interestingly, my edition of Baudelaire (1961) has the English translations of all the poems *in prose* alongside the originals; there is therefore no difference between the translated versions of the poems and the prose poems in this edition. But let us look more closely at the difference between the originals. There happen to be two poems in the Jeanne Duval cycle on the same subject: 'La Chevelure' ('Hair'), a poem consisting of seven cinquains and published in 1859, and 'Un Hémisphère dans une Chevelure', a prose poem of seven paragraphs published in 1862. Here is the opening stanza of the poem:

Ô toison, moutonnant jusque sur l'encolure!
Ô boucles! Ô parfum chargé de nonchaloir!
Extase! Pour peupler ce soir l'alcôve obscure
Des souvenirs dormant dans cette chevelure,
Je la veux agiter dans l'air comme un mouchoir!

and here the opening paragraph of the prose poem:

Laisse-moi respirer longtemps, longtemps, l'odeur de tes cheveux, y plonger tout mon visage, comme un homme altéré dans l'eau d'une source, et les agiter avec ma main comme un mouchoir odorant, pour secouer des souvenirs dans l'air

which could, of course, be made into three or five or six lines without affecting the nature of the work. The translation in my edition of the poem runs like this:

O Fleece, billowing down to the neck, O locks, O fragrance laden with languidness! O ecstasy! This night, to people the dark alcove of our love with all the memories that slumber in your hair, I long to wave it in the air as one waves a handkerchief.

Rendered in verse, it might read:

Your hair, breaking in waves on your neck!
Your mane! A perfume charged with carelessness!
Ecstasy! To crowd tonight the stable
Of memories sleeping in your hair,
I want to wave it in the air like a handkerchief.

There are at least three areas we are exploring here: first, the difference between the prose translation and the verse translation. Second, the question of what is lost in translation. Third, the difference between the original poem and the original prose poem. And so, more generally, the difference between poetry and prose.

First, the difference between the prose and verse translations. Clearly, the diction is different: the first is grander, more consciously 'romantic' than the second. It is also more 'accurate' in the sense of dictionary equivalence, but at the same time it distils the more sensual suggestion of the original, so that associations of horses that run through the French ('moutonnant' – breaking into white horses on the sea; 'encolure' – neck and withers of a horse) are lost, and become transposed to the more generalized 'fleece' and to 'billowing' – more like a sail. The diction (e.g. 'slumber') is more 'poetic'. The second translation is more down-to-earth, more 'modern', more consciously sensual, more 'prosaic' (ironically), and crucially, more rhythmic. Despite working some internal rhyming into the translation, it loses the ABAAB rhyming of the original; the function of that rhyme in the original is not only to create a mellifluousness, but also to point the rhythm of the poem. In the translated version, the mellifluousness is lost, but some attempt is made to retain the rhythmic identity of the original.

We can see from this discussion what is lost in the translation of poems: not only the 'correspondence' (Baudelaire's term) between the sounds and meanings of words, but also the rhythmic interdependence, the temporal relations of the whole. This is the second of the points to be made from this analysis. Third, having looked at the rhythmic identity of the opening of 'La Chevelure', what can be said about a comparison with the opening of 'Un Hémisphère dans une Chevelure'?

The imagery and tone of the two openings are remarkably similar. Both use the images of perfume and handkerchieves, and both suggest that a waving of the hair will release memories upon the air. Apart from that, what can we say about the rhythmic nature of the prose poem? Part of the difference is carried in the punctuation. The first stanza of the poem consists of five sentences, three of which end at the end of lines. The other two are brief declaratory utterances (Ô boucles!', 'Extase!'), the shortest of which immediately precedes the longest sentence in the stanza – the last one. Thus it is that a kind of irregular breathlessness is followed by release in this poetic stanza. Not so in the prose poem, where a single sentence comprises the whole of the first paragraph. It could be argued that this looser, more relaxed rhythm is entirely in keeping with the message being conveyed. In fact, if we look at the whole of 'Un Hémisphère dans une Chevelure', five of the seven paragraphs are like this first one in that they consist of one sentence. It begins to look as though each of the paragraphs is the equivalent of a line of poetry, and that Baudelaire's prose poems are closer to Whitman's verse in this respect than one would imagine.

Would it be fair to say, then, that prose poems are poems in which the usual parameters of the line of poetry are extended – the tension is relaxed – to any length, so that the poem begins to *look* like prose, even though it retains all the other qualities that we associate with poems, like compression, rhythmic identity, use of imagery and so on? Or, to come back to our earlier suggestion, should prose poems in fact be considered as a particular kind of prose and not be conflated with poems at all? Whichever line is taken, an important bridge is being built between poetry and prose here: one that has wider implications regarding the kinds of attitude that were outlined in the previous chapter, and one which will inform our thinking about the whole field of written discourse.

The discussion of the Baudelaire poems touched on the subject of 'translating' from poetry to prose and vice-versa. Let us look at this question from both angles: first from that of moving from poetic form to prose, and then at the transition from prose to poetry.

In the following poem, which is classically lyric,[1] what is lost if it is translated into prose?

> A slumber did my spirit seal;
>   I had no human fears:
> She seemed a thing that could not feel
> The touch of earthly years.
>
> No motion has she now, no force;
>   She neither hears nor sees;
> Rolled round in earth's diurnal course,
> With rocks, and stones, and trees.

Here is the prose version for immediate comparison:

> A slumber did my spirit seal; I had no human fears; she seemed a thing that could not feel the touch of earthly years. No motion has she now, no force; she neither hears nor sees; rolled round in earth's diurnal course, with rocks, and stones, and trees.

Perhaps the immediate points to mention are that despite the shift into prose, the rhythm is clearly pointed by the rhyme ('seal', 'fears', 'feel' and 'years' etc.) and so it hardly reads like 'normal' prose. The iambic tetrameter of the first and third line in each stanza and the iambic trimeter of the second and fourth ('ballad rhythm') shine through the prose; in fact, the punctuation mirrors this rhythmic pattern on the whole. Only at the end of the third line, where there is no punctuation, and in the first and fourth lines of the second stanza, where there are extra commas (perhaps to slow down a reading) does the punctuation not exactly mirror the rhythmic patterning of the poem. The difference between the two versions is obvious visually, so that what the poem does make clear is the rhythmic patterning we have been describing. But it also does more. If a poem is 'a story set down ways', what we are presented with is a series of lines, each a self-contained statement, which sit in some kind of parallel relationship to each other. Instead of the logical narrative drive of the prose account, which either has a chronological or logical significance, one statement following another and *modifying* it; instead of that arrangement we have one in which the phrases and lines are moved out of chronological, but not entirely out of logical sequence. The rhythm has lifted them out of time but also changed their relationship to each other. Now the lines and stanzas (in which there is a change of tense) are arrayed, made parallel, given the opportunity for maximum interrelatedness: one experience is compared to another, and defined in relation to its context, not in relation to some arbitrary chronological standard.

Is there a difference when we consider free verse, i.e. verse 'unfettered' by metre, but which still has rhythmic shape? Whitman's poetry, already mentioned, is free in this sense in that there is no regular metre informing the development of the lines; the lines vary in length, from less than a 'line' of the page in length to several lines. And yet the characteristic quality of Whitman's rhythms comes from the relationship between these lines in the poem as a whole.

Here is another, very different, example of free verse:

Fresh Water

They say it is very difficult
to distil sea-water into sweet.

Perhaps that's why it is so difficult
to get a refreshing drink out of old wisdom
old truth, old teaching of any sort.
                                (D. H. Lawrence)

Despite the brevity and the discursive quality of the poem, this has one element in common with the Whitman lines quoted earlier in the chapter: that the rhythm is 'flat' in relation to a poem by H. D. or Pound, writing at about the same time. This makes the poem an interesting case to discuss, however. What can be said about its form? First, that it is unquestionably a poem according to all the definitions cited so far in this book. Second, that it divides into two sections, each of which has a fairly consistent line-length. The first section (or 'strophe' or 'paragraph' – we cannot call it a 'stanza' or 'verse') consists of two lines of nine syllables each, and the second of three lines of ten, twelve and nine syllables respectively. We are not sure that syllabic length is significant at this point, but for the sake of the argument, let us pursue it for the moment. It does not commit us to any rhythmic pattern based on quantity or stress. We can depict this structural relationship in order to see it clearly:

Syllabically, there is a basic pattern in this poem: that of the line of nine syllables. The fact that the poem starts by establishing this pattern, and then comes back to it as an act of closure after the two longer lines may not be insignificant.

Third, does the syllabic patterning suggest any rhythmic identity? It is hard to perceive much rhythmical shaping in this poem, except for the echoing of the pattern of 'old wisdom' in the penultimate line by 'old truth, old teaching' in the final one. In fact, the rhythmical shape of 'Fresh Water' is defined not by the lines as much as by the two sections, the second of which exceeds the first in Fibonacci proportion. You can't scan this poem in the way you could notate Pound's 'The Return', which approximates music more than speech.

Fourth, how does the punctuation and sentence structure stand in relation to the visual and aural patterning of the poem?[2] It follows the structure of the paragraphs exactly. There is no complicating cross-rhythm, no pausing other than at the end of the sections except between the second and third rhythmical units noted above, 'old truth, old teaching'. This is an interesting feature, because of all the line-endings (which we would expect to carry some temporal weight), only the fourth, 'old wisdom' suggests a pause – largely because in the normal syntax of English prose, we would expect one there anyway.

To summarize so far, we can say that this poem's form is determined by syllable length and section relationship, supported by sentence structure, rather than by any repetitive rhythmic quality (except within those last two lines). It is closer to the rhythm of prose than those of poetry, and yet it remains a poem by virtue of its shape. Its subject matter, imagery and tenor are self-evident and match the pattern described: image (first section) + tenor (second); its diction colloquial.

What about the transition from prose to poetry? We know from accounts by Yeats and others that some writers draft in prose before moving into poetic form. What are the significant points of transition from one mode to the other? Here is an example of a prose draft (that in itself emerged from scribbled notes put down anywhere on a page):

> When I was thirteen I lived on the streets; lamp posts, cars and bikes were my landscape. I spent all my time looking at people. Animals, trees and fields I left behind in another country. I did not speak the language of my parents. Old parts of me spoke that language. Other parts of me communicated with my brothers and sisters, even ones I didn't have. But most of my language was inside me. I was learning a new language.

Putting aside the changes made to the wording of the text, what changes in the patterning of the experience have taken place by the time we reach a draft of the *poem*?

> When I was thirteen
> I lived on the streets:
> lamp posts, cars and bikes
> were my landmarks.
> I spent all my time looking at people.
> Animals, trees and fields
> I left behind in another country.
> There was no book to guide me.
> I relied on instinct,
> often riding no hands down back lanes,

through traffic. I did not read
the signs. I did not speak
the language of my parents.
Who did I talk to? Brothers,
sisters I never had. But
most of my language was inside me.
I was learning a new language.

We can see that there is a conscious or unconscious limitation to the length of the poetic line operating. No single line is more than eight words long, and none shorter than three words. Visually, there is a rough uniformity to the poem: the left hand margin remains constant, while the right stays within certain limits. What is the informing principle of this standard line? Each line, it seems, represents a grammatical snapshot, a segment of meaningful text. The first one, for instance, 'When I was thirteen' acts as a kind of setting, placing the experiences described in time; the third, 'lamp posts, cars and bikes', lists the constituents of the new landscape. There would be no point, within this poem, in breaking up that last line into two or three parts, unless particular emphasis was to be placed on each of the items in the poem as a whole. At the same time, each line represents – or acts as a notation of – a breath. So that there is a dual notation system operating in the poem: that of conventional punctuation (which is also there in the prose version) and that of the length and relative positioning of the poetic lines. This double notation means that most readings of the poem will be slower than the readings of the prose. Let's look in particular at the last seven lines of the poem. The conventional ordering of the sentences is deliberately (we assume) broken up by the rhythm, so that there is a kind of limping effect created. If, in 'practical criticism' terms, we are looking to establish a unity in the poem, we might suggest that this in turn reflects the stumbling towards a new language, the difficulty in expression that the thirteen-year-old is experiencing, and that as such it is an entirely appropriate way to arrange the words. It is certainly true that this dimension of the meaning is totally lacking from the prose draft. And yet the last line asserts the reunification of the rhythms of the poem with the orderliness of the syntax and sentence structure, as if some kind of reconciliation has taken place.

But how can we describe the rhythm generated in this poem? It seems to operate against no absolute pattern or metre, but to establish itself as it goes along; it seems, therefore, to be additive and relative rather than regular and absolute. As much twentieth century poetry comes in this mode, and particularly as much writing by students in school also takes this form, we must try to account for its rhythms.

Problems of prosody

You will see how bothered I am when I get to prosody – because it is the most certain of my instincts, it is the subject of which I am most ignorant.
(W. B. Yeats, in a letter to Edith Shackleton Head, August, 1937)

Part of the problem with poetry is that there is no adequate modern prosody. Consequently, we find it hard to talk about the range of rhythms in contemporary verse. And as a further consequence, we don't talk about it and begin to rule it out of our sensibility. And because poetry is so implicated with rhythm, poetry goes too.

We can, however, make a start on tackling this problem, and in doing so will draw heavily on the practice and thinking about rhythm of some notable free-verse writers this century: William Carlos Williams, Eliot, Lawrence, Octavio Paz and most importantly, Ezra Pound.

Let us first test the hypothesis that the 'line' of poetry – the rhythmical unit in free verse and perhaps in all verse – is determined in length by the poet's 'breath'. If so, we can expect a line with fewer syllables in it to be proportionately longer in the value it places on those syllables than a line with more syllables in it. Putting aside tempo, the weight of the potential lines in a poem will be the same, but their actual weight relative to each other will vary. It is interesting, at this point, to consider what 'standard' length of line various poets work to: Carlos Williams writes a generally shorter line than Pound, and in turn, Bunting is shorter than both of them. All three are shorter than Whitman.

Williams talks about his own rhythmic pattern in a letter to Richard Eberhart (23rd May 1954, reprinted in the Penguin *Critical Anthology*, ed. Charles Tomlinson, p. 313):

> I have never been one to write by rule, even by my own rules. Let's begin with the rule of counted syllables, in which all poems have been written hitherto. That has become tiresome to my ear.
>
> Finally, the stated syllables, as in the best of present-day free verse, have become entirely divorced from the beat, that is the measure. The musical pace proceeds without them.
>
> Therefore the measure, that is to say the count, having got rid of the words, which held it down, is returned to the music.
>
> The words, having been freed, have been allowed to run all over the map, 'free', as we have mistakenly thought. This has amounted to no more (in Whitman and others) than no discipline at all.
>
> But if we keep in mind the tune which the lines (not necessarily the words) make in our ears, we are ready to proceed.
>
> By measure I mean musical pace. Now, with music in our ears the words need only to be taught to keep as distinguished an order, as chosen a character, as regular according to the music, as in the best prose . . .
>
> To give you an example from my own work – not that I know anything myself about what I have written:
>
> (1) The smell of the heat is boxwood
>   (2) when rousing us
>   (3) a movement of the air
>   (4) stirs our thoughts
>   (5) that had no life in them
>   (6) to a life, a life in which

Count with a single beat to each numeral. You may not agree with my ear, but that is the way I count the line. Over the whole poem it gives the pattern to the meter that can be felt as a new measure. It gives resources to the ear which result in a language which we hear spoken about us every day.

There is much here that is derivative of Pound in the best sense – the breaking away from traditional English metres, the emphasis on 'measure' (cf. dance) or rhythm. But what is distinctively Williams' own formulation is the notion of relativity and the associations with 'measure'. While Pound talks about 'absolute rhythm' (by which he means that there is a definite and uncontrovertible rhythm for each network of feelings and thoughts, *not* that metres and rhythms are determined by some absolute measure), Williams draws on Einstein:

> When Einstein promulgated the theory of relativity he could not have foreseen . . . its influence on the writing of poetry
>
> (*Selected Letters*, p. 335)

and, perhaps more usefully,

> The first thing you learn when you begin to learn anything about this earth is that you are eternally barred save from the report of your senses from knowing anything about it. *Measure serves for us as the key*: we can measure between objects; therefore we know that they exist. (my italics)

There is a connection, then, between our 'measurements' of the world (the term, coming from a doctor, is doubly powerful) and the 'measures' of verse. We 'measure' with metaphor (a measurement of scale) and rhythm (a measure in time). In a theoretical and general sense, Williams has keyed in to a connection between rhythm and observation that is less emphatic in other poets.

Williams, like Pound, uses the typographical setting of his poems to indicate the exact 'measure' between the several phrases that make up the poem; as Olson observes, the typewriter could

> indicate exactly the breath, the pauses, the suspensions even of syllables, the juxtaposition even of parts of phrases
>
> ('Projective verse vs. Non-Projective' in *Poetry New York*, No. 3, 1950)

I am probably inclined to agree with those that see Williams' theorizing and his practice as not being totally integrated. There is too much rigidity in the Williams line for the measures to be analogous to measurements between objects in the world. If anything, the old metres are replaced by a new rhythmical norm, despite talk about a 'variable foot'. On the other hand, to suggest as Alan Stephens does in his review of *Pictures from Breughel* (in *Poetry*, Vol. 101, No. 5, 1963), that

> The general principle is this: a line is a line because, relative to the neighbouring lines, it contains that which makes it in its own right a unit of the attention . . . The norm is the ordinary unit of the attention in language – the formal architecture of the sentence . . . If this is so, then audible rhythm, whether produced by a formal metric

or by improvisation, is not the supreme fact of the verse line (though it is of course indispensable)

is to miss the point. There seems to me no need to split the rhythmic unit from the unit of attention; indeed, as suggested in the analysis of the poem translated from prose above, this is the very combination that goes towards making poetry a distinct form of discourse. We are clearer about that now that free verse has exposed the line to analysis, isolating it from its embedded position in stanzas and regular metres.

Before we get on to Pound's contribution to the question of rhythm in poetry, it is worth exploring the context in which Pound's insights about rhythm took place. As Yeats' secretary for a time, Pound was well aware of the 'master's' sensitivity 'to a limited gamut of rhythms' (in the 'Treatise on Metre' 1951b: p. 198). One (apocryphal?) anecdote from the Stone Cottage period tells how Pound retired early one night, leaving Yeats downstairs. Later, a resonating hum seemed to come up the chimney. When Pound went down to see what it was, he saw Yeats, with eyes half-closed, intoning and composing in front of the fire. This is 'music just forcing itself into articulate speech', an expression of what Rémy de Gourmont called – and Pound was fond of quoting – 'the unspoken words of my body'. We can see Yeats' own contention that man can *embody* truth, but not know it, more clearly now, and appreciate the distinction described by Yeats in his letter to Edith Shackleton Head (quoted earlier). There are many other aspects of the relationship between Pound and Yeats which reveal a common interest in rhythm.

D. H. Lawrence, too, had much to say about this phenomenon. In the introduction to the American edition of *New Poems*, he talks about 'the poetry of the instant':

> From the beginning it is obvious that the poetry of the instant present cannot have the same body or the same motion as the poetry of the before and after . . . It is never finished. There is no rhythm which returns upon itself, no serpent of eternity with its tail in its own mouth. There is no static perfection, none of that finality which we find so satisfying because we are so frightened.

This is a problematic position, because the very nature of rhythm is based on the principle of repetition, however freely that repetition is interpreted. Like Whitman's, Lawrence's free verse is predicated on a line unit that often extends for much greater length than usual; it is a verse which moves further away from music than the work of Pound, Eliot or any of their French forebears. But it shares the release from the strictly repetitive metres of the neo-Georgian school. What is particularly interesting about Lawrence's formulation, though, is the association of the freer rhythms with poetry of the *instant*. This is an alternative version of the theory that rhythm 'defeats' the supposed 'linear' passage of time by setting up patterns that enable us to compare experiences/thoughts/feelings. This may well be as true of narratives (on a larger scale) as it seems to be of poetry, but in Lawrence's free verse at least, the attempt is to capture the present by recourse to free verse. It is clear from the statement quoted above that this enterprise is very different from the conventional approach, which is characterized as 'the poetry of the before and after'.

The same sense of the function of rhythm is found in Lévi-Strauss, but here applied to myth, music and dreaming, which are 'machines for the suppression of time' (*Mythologiques*, I, Paris 1964: p. 24). According to Edmund Leach (1970) in his book on Lévi-Strauss,

> The repetitions and thematic variations of a musical score produce responses in the listener which depend in some way on his physiological rhythms; and in like measure ... the repetitions and thematic variations of myth play upon physiological characters of the human brain to produce emotional as well as purely intellectual effects.

And the beginning of Octavio Paz's essay, 'Recapitulations' (op. cit. 1974: p. 65), echoes this sense of the framing and rearranging of time that rhythm seems to effect. The first statement is redolent of Yeats:

> The poem is unexplainable, not unintelligible.
> A poem is rhythmic language – not language with a rhythm (song) or mere verbal rhythm (a property common to all language, including prose).
> Rhythm is the relation of difference and similarity: this sound is *not* that one, this sound is *like* that one.
> Rhythm is the original metaphor and encompasses all the others. It says: succession is repetition, time is nontime.
> Whether lyric, epic, or dramatic, the poem is succession and repetition, a date on the calendar and a rite. The 'happening' is also a poem (theater) and a rite (fiesta) but it lacks one essential element: rhythm.

This is the element alluded to in the epigraph to this chapter, from Herrnstein Smith's book, *Poetic Closure* (1968), in which she affirms the 'ahistorical' nature of the poem (p. 15). The initial pages of that book (pp. 4–5) are at pains to point out that although 'the sense of closure is a function of the perception of structure',

> The principles of poetic and musical structure are comparable only insofar as both forms of art produce experiences which occur over a period of time and are continuously modified by successive events. Because language, however, has semantic or symbolic as well as physical properties, poetic structure is considerably more complex,

so that any extrapolation from music to poetry is limited. Nevertheless, at the level of structure, the analogy has informed much twentieth century thought on the subject of accounting for the origin, shape and effects of poetry.

Eliot (1933), for instance, in describing the 'auditory imagination', talks about

> the feeling for syllable and rhythm, penetrating far below the conscious levels of thought and feeling, invigorating every word; sinking to the most primitive and forgotten . . . It works through meanings in the ordinary sense, and fuses the old and

obliterated and the trite, the current, and the new and surprising, the most ancient and the most civilized mentality.

And elsewhere, in a justly memorable passage, he writes:

I know that a poem, or a passage of a poem, may tend to realize itself first as a particular rhythm before it reaches expression in words, and that this rhythm may bring to birth the idea and the image; and I do not believe this is an experience peculiar to myself.

Enough has been said to suggest that rhythmic form and considerations of the sources and functions of rhythm in poetry were a preoccupation for many of the major poets of the early part of the century. What are the reasons for this interest in rhythm? Why does it form such an important part of the poetic?

There are various features of rhythm, as opposed to other musical elements like tone, pitch and tempo, which seem particularly appropriate to poetry and also to its twentieth-century milieu. These are its primitiveness, its association with physicality and with dance and movement, its choreographing of temporal relations. Poetry's move to break away from the pentameter, to follow French example and frame the rhythmic relations of words in terms of quantity rather than beat, to further explore 'vers libre' in looking at the relative periods between words and phrases rather than at a regular metrical foundation to them – all these moves had a good deal in common with moves in musical history like Stravinsky's use of complex time signatures, the interest in jazz, and the search for new forms of notation.

In a letter to Mary Barnard in 1934, Pound (1951a: p. 254) recognized his debt to music:

The only book of any use on rhythm is Greek section in Vol. I *Encyclopédie de la Musique*, Laurence et Lavignac . . . I know nothing else of any use . . . What they call 'solfège' or 'savoir divider une note' is the job . . . Precision in knowing how long the different notes take in a given place . . . There aren't any rules. Thing is to cut a shape in time. Sounds that stop the flow, and durations either of syllables, or implied between them, 'forced onto the voice' of the reader by nature of the verse.

Pound's contribution to the increased awareness of rhythm in poetry is major, both through his own verse and through his writings on the subject. A proper examination of this contribution warrants an entire book; and although Pound's perceptions about the nature and function of rhythm are central to the thesis of *this* book, we must limit ourselves to a few key elements in his thinking.

Essential to the whole Poundian edifice is the notion that rhythm is the foundation of musical as well as poetic variation. In discussing the relationship between pitch and rhythm in 'A Treatise on Metre', he refers to Yeats again (1951b: pp. 197–8).

There is great laxity or vagueness permitted the poet in regard to pitch. He may be as great a poet as Mr Yeats and still think he doesn't know one note from another. Mr Yeats [who was apparently tone-deaf] probably could distinguish between a G and a

Bflat, but he is happy to think that he doesn't; and he would certainly be incapable of whistling a simple melody in tune. Nevertheless before writing a lyric he is apt to get 'a chune in his head'. He is very sensitive to a limited gamut of rhythms. Rhythm is a form cut into TIME, as a design is determined SPACE. A melody is a rhythm in which the pitch of each element is fixed by the composer (pitch: the number of vibrations per second).

That is to say, even pitch is a product of the relationship of intervals in time. Notice, too, the emphatic 'rhythm is a form cut into TIME, as a design is determined SPACE'. It was partly in reaction to the 'imprecise' rhythms of late nineteenth and early twentieth century poetry that Pound developed this passion for clarity, for clear-cut lines and precision regarding the shaping of the words on the page and in the air. Furthermore, rhythm acts as a metaphor for clarity of thought, and more importantly, *feeling*. In fact, Pound's belief, as already indicated, was in 'an ultimate and absolute rhythm' to express any emotional/ intellectual complex: for Pound, the emotions were carried in the rhythm, and the intellectual dimension in the word or *image*. This 'absolute rhythm' was not a single rhythmic phrase that was the *primum mobile* for all others, but one that fitted perfectly the 'emotion or shade of emotion to be expressed. A man's rhythm must be interpretive, it will be therefore, in the end, his own, uncounterfeiting, uncounterfeitable.' (1954: p. 9).

The important shift in attitude to rhythm evidenced here could not have taken place had rhythm still maintained its subservient role in relation to the other elements of music that had been the case in western music for some time. Releasing rhythm from this subservient position – and indeed, raising it to perhaps the principal position in the musical and poetic toolkit/repertoire – allows it not only to determine the message of the poem in more sensitive and organic ways; it also enables it to act as prime mover for all the other elements of music. Note, for example, the symphonic variation and colour of Stravinsky's ballet music as compared with the rhythmic virtuosity and historical and tonal range of the *Cantos*.

Let us not get rhythm out of perspective, though. Despite its centrality to Pound's poetic (and that of our own), it still remains but a feature of poetic composition. For all his enthusiasm, Pound is quite clear about this in '20th August 1917' and in *Literary Essays*:

> I think one must write *vers libre* only when one 'must', that is to say, only when the 'thing' builds up a rhythm more beautiful than that set of metres, or more real, more a part of the emotion of the 'thing', more germane, more intimate, interpretive than the measure of accentual verse; a rhythm that discontents one with set iambic or set anapestic.
>
> Eliot had said the thing very well when he said 'no *vers* is *libre* for the man who wants to do a good job'.

A classic of *vers libre* is Pound's poem 'The Return' from *Ripostes* (1912). This is the poem which Yeats described as 'the most beautiful poem that has been written in the free-form, one of the few in which I find real organic rhythm' and in which Hugh Kenner thinks that 'it is actually the rhythm that defines the meaning'. It begins with these four lines:

> See, they return; ah, see the tentative
> Movements, and the slow feet,
> The trouble in the pace and the uncertain
> Wavering!

What kind of prosody can account for this poem's rhythm? It is hard to define any kind of regular metre beneath the surface, let alone more audible in the movement of the words. Those who suggest that *vers libre* always takes as its point of reference a regular metre of some kind can hardly argue their case here. Is there, nevertheless, a recognizable pattern of stresses? There *is* a pattern of stresses: you might agree or disagree with this reading, but it seems to me that the pattern is as follows (allowing for two levels of stress, strong and weak);

/   ˘   ˘/   ˘ /   ˘ /   ˘ ˘
See, they return; ah, see the tentative

/   ˘   ˘ ˘ / /
Movements, and the slow feet,

˘ / ˘   ˘ ˘   /   ˘   ˘ ˘ / ˘
The trouble in the pace and the uncertain

/ ˘ ˘
Wavering!

Is this an adequate reading? What would happen if we read it in terms of quantity instead of stress, and expressed the prosody in musical notation?

♩ ♫ ♩ ♩ ♩ ♫
See, they return; ah, see the tentative

♩. ♩ ♩ ♩ ♩. ♩.
Movements, and the slow feet,

♩ ♫ ♫ ♩. ♫ ♩♩♩
The trouble in the pace and the uncertain

♩ ♫
Wavering!

(You might disagree with this particular reading, and experiment with your own versions.)

It is impossible to account for the rhythms of free verse purely in terms of quantity, of syllabic length. Not only is this evident from the analysis of the opening lines of 'The Return', but this is a generally held view amongst prosodists. Despite Pound's embracing of quantitative principles – largely because of their proximity to and correspondence with music – there are other features of rhythm which have to be taken into account. Let it be said, however, that Pound's position is not analogous to that of the early metrists in English who tried to impose classical patterns upon English speech and poetry: the accessibility of such quantitative rhythmic approaches to prescription in the form of rhetorical manuals was not part of Pound's enterprise at all. On the contrary, his approach was to attend to the music in word patterns and also to music *per se* as a training for the writing of verse.

The great advantage of Pound's approach, however unscientific it is, is that it can account in some way for the vagaries of free verse in a way that traditional (i.e. stress-based prosodies) cannot. Rather than there being posited some 'foot' or similar stress-unit as the basic unit of rhythm (an approach more suited to metrical analysis than to the study of rhythm), the quantitative/musical approach sees the line as the basic unit. As we have already suggested, a line of poetry can be as short as a punctuation mark or as long as needs be; this does not affect the principle of there being a rhythmic identity to the line *in relation to the other lines in the composition*. Once the principle of the line as rhythmic unit has been established, analysis of the particular rhythm of the individual lines can proceed using all the armoury of prosody, i.e. by combining the quantitative approach with the stress-based approach.

The truth of the matter is that stress-based prosodies, which gained prominence in the eighteenth and particularly in the nineteenth centuries, assume a certain regularity to the rhythm. Despite the wealth of rhetorical devices exhibited by these prosodies (the English stresses being grafted on to the classical terminologies), any combination of iambs, dactyls and anapaests is unable to account for the rhythmic complexity of the free verse line, just as the conventional bar notation in music, adequate to a composer like Chopin whose genius is primarily melodic, is stretched when it has to describe the rhythmic virtuosity of a Stravinsky. This is particularly the case because these accentual prosodies are usually based on the identification of only two stresses – 'strong' and 'weak' – and as such do not begin to reflect the number of stress levels observable in English speech or poetry; nor do these prosodies take full account of the temporal dimension to stress and accent.

Because prosodists and poet-critics have tried to account for Poundian free verse using the conventional apparatus of accentual metrics, they have persisted in seeing it as defined in some way in relation to some system of regulation, some kind of metric. Statements like 'Behind Pound's *Cantos* run a ghostly iambic' and 'the characteristics trochaic ending to Pound's lines' are, in my view, vain attempts to pull the verse back in line with an old order, or to see it as an aberration. Eliot's conservatism is evident in his stand on this question in his critique of *vers libre*

> ... freedom is only truly freedom when it appears against the background of an artificial limitation,

despite the rhythmic experimentation of the work from *Ash Wednesday* onwards which Helen Gardner so ably surveys in *The Art of T. S. Eliot*.

It seems futile to pursue the debate as to whether accentual *or* quantitative theories are best equipped to account for the varieties of verse. It would probably be fairly true to say that the former were better able to describe metrically based poetry, and that the latter were better placed to account for free verse, even though a combination of approaches is necessary to account for the whole rhythmic effect. But traditional approaches like these fall short of being able to provide a satisfactory prosody for free verse, because they do not take full account of the line.

What has been emerging during this chapter, both in the analysis of the differences between prose and poetry, and in the survey of attitudes towards rhythm by poets, musicians and prosodists this century, is that the notion of the 'line' as the defining characteristic of poetry is a central one.

Not only does the 'line' have a distinct rhythmic identity in relation to all the other lines in the poem, it also stands as a unit of sense as an alternative to the sentence. The particular power of this formulation is that we can lay the unit of sense alongside the unit of rhythm and begin to record the correspondences between the two. This two-fold combination of meaning and rhythm may be overlain by other 'poetic' features, like alliteration, assonance etc., but these are secondary to the work, and certainly not solely the province of poetry.

An added strength of this hypothesis is that it applies equally well to metrical verse as to free verse. What we have done is simply stretched the rhythmical unit from the accentual or quantitative 'foot' to the line as a whole, thus moving to a slightly higher unit within the discourse. And in doing so, we have revealed a further strength of this approach: that as well as the individual lines of a poem being laid alongside each other, as it were, for definition and comparison in rhythmic terms, there is a correspondent parallelling of sense that is unlike anything we encounter in prose. Indeed, the very 'breaking up' of continuously reported experience into these rhythmic and sense units called 'lines' involves a radically different perception of their interrelatedness than is the case in prose, where one episode acts as the springboard for the next. This is, of course, stating the case of poetry in relation to and as some kind of secondary version of prose, which is not the overall intention. They stand as equally valid forms of discourse, and it is part of the purpose of this book to accord poetry its status in this respect.

How all this applies to what children write and read in and beyond school will be made clear in Chapters 6–8; but before we turn to more practical matters, we should look at two further areas that are problematic in poetry, namely the limitations of the canon and the social construction of poetry.

Notes

1 The poem is the subject of a discussion between Hillis Miller and Abrams, reviewed in *New York Review of Books* by Robert M. Adams, Vol. XXXVII, No. 3, March 1st 1990, p. 38.

2 A feature of poetry identified by Veronica Forrest-Thomson in her *Poetic Artifice* (1978)
  makes it clearly distinguishable from prose: 'The most important level to destroy is the
  syntactic. For it is through syntax – the suggestion that a coherent proposition is being
  offered – that external meaning smothers words.' We could add that prose, when it
  employs rhythm, tends to use it to enhance or support the syntactical patterns of speech
  or prose; but that in poetry, rhythm can not only support and enhance, but can also
  operate against the syntactic flow as well as using its markers – like rhyme, alliteration
  etc. – to point or define the relationship between rhythm and meaning.

5 Poetry in context

... every word uttered by the lyric voice sets a limit, announces the inability of that voice to say all there is to say; it is this limit which resonates.

David Trotter on Paul Celan

The last chapter focused on the texts of poetry; this one looks at its contexts. There are three sections to the chapter: the first looks at the British poetic in political and international perspective; the second explores the nature of the anthology, the most popular format for poems in schools; and the third reviews the kinds of approaches to writing poetry in schools, and aims to set them in relation to each other.

The British poetic

The prevailing poetic in Britain sees poetry – as it does fiction – as *escape*. We read poems to retreat and reflect upon ourselves and our relations with the world. So much of this position is taken for granted that it is worth unpacking these assumptions. The common assumption is that we read in 'spectator' role; we are temporarily disengaged from the action of the world when we read. The language we interpret and entertain in our minds is not the language of transactions, not the language of 'getting things done'. Rather, it is a self-possessed, self-referring language; we enjoy it 'for itself'. And because of the peculiar predication of the self in our culture, we see this activity as a 'retreat' from the world. Poetry in particular seems to inhabit an island – a pleasant, orderly island – in a sea of troubles.

One of the interesting aspects of reading poetry is that we usually read poems in groups: to continue the island metaphor, they are archipelagos which come in slim volumes by individual authors, in anthologies of various persuasions with poems by other writers, or in large collected volumes; if we attend readings, we hear them in clusters. Only on rare posters or on 'Poems on the Underground' – or perhaps at weddings and funerals and other special occasions – are we likely to see or hear them singly. This means that a poem is usually flanked by other poems; its context is almost always literary.

Such contextualizing is only possible because the poems in question are *short*. It is difficult and pointless trying to determine the average length of poems in the late twentieth century, but the dominance of the lyric has meant that we expect poems to cover less than a page. With a few notable exceptions – 'The Waste Land', *The Cantos*, 'Briggflatts', the poems of James Merrill and others – the prevailing impulse is lyric; the reflective dimension extends the poem somewhat. Epic and large-scale narrative structures are the exception rather than the rule; in most cases, those functions have been taken over by the novel.

The organizing principle of volumes of poems, however, is usually thematic: books of poems carry titles like *From Glasgow to Saturn* or *Barbarians*. These titles may also be the title of one of the poems in the collection, but they carry resonance within the collection as a whole. The point is that the individual poem is set within this cluster of related poems by virtue of its inclusion in a book. This is true even if poems are often first published in magazines, either flanked by other poems or by other kinds of texts.

A further identifying feature of poetry within our culture is that it tends to be seen as the product of a single 'voice'. Poems, like novels and short stories, are thought to be the work of individuals, unlike some plays and other less 'personal' texts (both fictional and non-fictional). Like most works of fiction – with the exception of film – they carry the imprint of the individual artist. This feature of poetry is closely connected to the legacies of the romantic tradition discussed in Chapter 3. Even Pound's massive contribution to the structuring and shaping of 'The Waste Land' is seen as minimal compared to the expressive contribution of Eliot. It is easy to forget that 'voice' in writing is a metaphor drawn from speech; in concrete terms, its manifestation in poetic texts is probably carried most sensitively in the rhythmic structures and modulations of the poem.

The emphasis on 'voice', on the expression of the single self, is linked to the notion that poetry conveys *feeling*. There is no doubt that it does, and it seems the case in most poems that the feeling is embodied or potential within the rhythms. Pound's formulation that the feeling of the poem is carried in the rhythm and the intellectual content in the imagery is firmly within this camp. But despite Eliot's drawing our attention to the 'dissociation of sensibility' – the perception of a split between feeling and thought – many of us still associate poetry with feelings *rather than* thoughts. It is as if we believe that the poem appeals to an area of our sensibilities that is divorced from other areas; it can have no political power because it is the expression of personal feelings, and as such operates on a different plane. It is private rather than public.

This *privacy* is another aspect of the British poetic; poetry almost takes on a covert function within our society, so closely is it associated with the private 'inner' life of people. At times it verges on the subversive, but only when it breaks out of its private enclave and begins to operate in the world.

We can take this crudely sketched outline of the British poetic further. It might be projected that a poetry that embodies the private expression of feeling, that is associated with escape and that is usually lyric in impulse would be celebratory if not exultant. Some of it is. But the largest proportion of adult poetry published and written is melancholic in tone. This may be the inevitable result of its reflectiveness ('emotion *recollected* in tranquillity' sums up much of what we have been depicting about the British poetic), with its looking back, often to rosier states, or its lamenting some event or present thinning of experience.

It is odd that British poetry should have locked itself into this mode. There is a poetry that tries to capture the present, and in doing so is dramatic, slippery and inspirational in a way that prose can hardly ever be. Lawrence's free verse, with its conscious emphasis on thoughts ('pansies' = 'pensées') and his writing about 'the poetry of the instant' come into this category; the writing of Voznesensky ('Nostalgia for the Present') and other Russian and East European poets; James Berry's carnival poems which manage to capture the exciting physicality of movement in words; Tony Harrison's political and fiercely contemporary verse – all these are possible ways of writing poetry that only serve to highlight the general picture. It is probably not unfair to say that much British poetry is too safe, too clever, too limited in its scope and context to have much lasting significance, or to excite the imaginations and ears of children in schools.

Bowra (1966) is critical of this insularity in his lectures delivered at Queen's University, Belfast, in 1965. In exploring the history of political poetry he refers to the Greeks, Dante, Milton and the poets of the Romantic age – not mentioning Shakespeare, Marvell, Dryden and others, all of whom establish a strong lineage for political poetry in English and European traditions. If there is any doubt about this, Tom Paulin's anthology of political verse (1986) will allay it.

Paulin attacks the 'aristocratic, hierarchical conservative tradition which Arnold and T. S. Eliot have floated as the major cultural hegemony in these islands' (p. 15), seeing a calculated obliteration of 'the Protestant prophetic tradition' (p. 16). It is this rediscovery of a popular tradition in political poetry that is one of the main strands of *The Faber Book of Political Verse*, and it informs a broad conception of what constitutes 'political verse' (p. 18):

> my definition of a political poem does not assume that such poems necessarily make an ideological statement. They can instead embody a general historical awareness – an observation of the rain – rather than offering a specific attitude to a state of affairs.

What we get in the anthology itself is a sense of the language freed from aesthetic confines, and so more transparent in nature and influential in effect. These are poems which set out not only to 'turn the mind around' via the operation of feeling, but also to act as a spur to action.

One important point to emerge from a consideration of the history of the relationship between poetry and politics is that the very poets who are supposed to be the perpetrators of the Romantic tradition in poetry – which, on first sight, would seem to lend support to the notion that poetry is a private, self-searching, imagistic, formally conservative practice – are in fact some of the most politically aware and *active* poets that we have had. One only has to think of Byron in Greece, Wordsworth's involvement in the French revolution and Blake's allegorical diatribes to be convinced of this; and one can then see that it is not these 'high' romantics, but the distillations of romanticism in the latter half of the nineteenth century and the first half of the twentieth that have given rise to the notion of the artist in isolation, the work that speaks for itself, the consequent irrelevance of poetry to the affairs of the world in our poetic.

In particular, Bowra traces the transition from the conservatism and security of the late Victorian period which generated a public poetry that was conventional and passionate, to a private poetic which struggles to meet public issues. Poems like 'The Charge of the Light Brigade' and even Hopkins' 'Tom's Garland', written in 1887 about the unemployed, speaking from a position of settled values and authority: they express a generalized emotion on behalf of the people, but it is a conventional, 'safe' expression. There is little in the way of argument. Nothing happens as a result of the poems, and ideas come second to the expression of acceptable feelings. Kipling's work (though both his and Hopkins' poetry are much more complex than is suggested here) continues this tradition, which finds its logical extension in the bankrupt propaganda of Newbolt and the naive hopefulness of the early Brooke. The way the war is handled by Sassoon and Rosenberg is seen as an antidote to this line of development, but the particular perspective of the war poets is revealed as being a very personal response to a public theme. At a further extreme is the position of Eliot, for whom the war poets are 'occasional poets' and for whom 'War is not a life; it is a situation'. His is a case of a private sensibility registering the climate of the age but not directly dealing with public themes or issues.

For the purposes of the present book, there are two more important points that arise from Bowra's lectures, but which are not made explicit in them. The first is the connection between poetic form and the function of the poem; and the second is the international range of reference, which puts the British poetic into sharper perspective.

It is worth noting that, in general, romantic expression is couched in conventional poetic forms like the sonnet, the ode, the ballad, the dramatic (blank verse) monologue; stanzas are often regular, the most popular being the quatrain and sestet; rhythms are usually stable, and most of the modulation is carried in the cadence of the words. The real break with this tradition is in the work of Pound, Eliot and the *imagistes* and *symbolistes*, whose 'breaking of the pentameter' and exploration of collage, free verse, different voices and more syncopated and 'jazz' rhythms coincides with a more introspective stand in relation to subject matter and audience. What happens when the subject matter is more public, when the voice takes on less of a private range, when the audience is assumed to be more directly on the other end of the message?

The poems may well continue to be couched in the traditional forms – on Yeats' principle that 'ancient salt is best packing' – but it is the larger-scale forms which tend to be used. The lyric impulse, which tends to favour the shorter forms (like the sonnet) or the narrative forms (narrative poem, ballad) is extended to fill forms like the ode, or longer sequences of stanzas. Length is necessary to give a fuller picture of the situation and especially to construct an argument. Narrative continues to play an important role.

What is particularly interesting is the change in rhythm and use of imagery when we look at political verse from other cultures. Pablo Neruda, the Chilean poet, communist and sometime ambassador for the country, begins a poem about the Spanish Civil War in the following way:

> Preguntaréis: Y dónde están las lilas?
> Y la metafísica cubierta de amapolas?
> Y la lluvia que a menudo golpeaba
> sus palabras llenándolas
> de agujeros y pájaros?

> (You will ask: and where are the lilacs?
> And the poppy-petalled metaphysics?
> And the rain continually strafing
> its words full
> of holes and birds?)

So much for conventional versifying. The aesthetic drive of poetry, represented in the flower imagery, the metaphysics and the 'rain of words' are replaced by a disarming straightforwardness:

> Os voy a contar todo lo que me pasa
> (I'll tell you what happened)

and then the poet proceeds to tell how one morning, all the calm and fecundity – its markets, flowers, houses – of his suburb of Madrid is shattered by an attack by 'bandidos' (bandits) who come to kill children and destroy the neighbourhood. There is a return to the rhetorical questioning of the poet by the reader/listener, asking why the poetry doesn't speak 'del sueño, del las hojas,/de los grandes volcanes de su país natal' ('of dreams, of the leaves,/of the great volcanoes of his native land'). Neruda's answer ('Come and see the blood on the streets') is repeated three times, in three different rhythmic modulations:

> Venid a ver la sangre por las calles.
> Venid a ver
> la sangre por las calles.
> Venid a ver la sangre
> por las calles!

Even in translation – where rhythm and image are likely to lose some of their distinctive character and redolence – the directness of poet speaking to listener/ reader (as if the poem were a conversation), the deliberate subversion of metaphor, the phrasing and blocking of the words and the fearless taking of a stand on a life-and-death political issue all come across strongly. The poem is called 'Explico algunas cosas' ('I'll explain a few things').

Some poets eschew metaphor altogether, belying the assumption that metaphor and simile are *the* identifying features of poetry. The true picture is that metaphor is a secondary, optional feature of poetry. Some of Brecht's work falls into this category, its function being to communicate as directly and effectively as possible rather than to 'hide' its meaning in figurative language:

> Please, doctor, I've missed my monthly . . .
> Why, this is simply great.
> If I may put it bluntly
> You're raising our birthrate.

The principal clue to the meaning(s) of this poem, 'The Ballad of Paragraph 218', is – as Voloshinov (1983) says of speech – *tone*. Like speech acts, these poems must be interpreted in their context; indeed, they read like speech. Moreover, the form underpinning both the Neruda and the Brecht is dialogue, and hence the beginnings of drama. All these qualities are untypical of British poetry, cut off as it is in the main from the political dimension.

This is not to say that all political poetry is direct, unmetaphorical, dialogic and rhythmically free. Metaphor, for example, can work to powerful effect in political verse just as it can in any verse. The work of Miroslav Holub in Czechoslovakia and Nicolás Guillén, the Cuban poet, are cases in point. Guillén published in 1967 a volume entitled *El Gran Zoo* (*The Great Zoo*) (Guillén 1972), in which he conducts the reader from cage to cage, introducing the 'exhibits' which range from objects ('The Atomic Bomb') through climatic phenomena ('The Winds', 'The Clouds') and creatures ('The Tiger') to people ('Gangster') and concepts ('Thirst', 'Hunger'). In effect, anything and anyone can find itself in the great zoo and so all these phenomena are metamorphosed into zoo creatures; the language of the poems is the clipped explanatory language of the plaque on the cage. This is the beginning of the poem 'Ciclón' ('Cyclone'):

> Ciclón de raza,
> recién llegado a Cuba de las islas Bahamas.
> (A thoroughbred cyclone,
> recently arrived in Cuba from the Bahamas.)

Indeed, there is nothing tonal in these poems; on the contrary, the collection is unified by a consistently flat expositional tone. What is striking is that an overall metaphor governs the collection, and this metaphor is both accessible and complex. It is eminently suitable for use with children at primary and secondary level as a way into using and learning about the function of metaphor. Variations of the principal metaphor, as well as the introduction of new metaphors, can take place in the individual poems, which can be overtly or covertly political.

Looking briefly at the possibilities offered by Neruda, Brecht and Guillén (all of whom happen to be mentioned in *Poetry and Politics 1900–1960*) brings us back to Bowra's contention at the end of his series of lectures. 'At the moment,' he claims (p. 137),

> poetry is not read so much as it has been in the past, and though there are many reasons for this, one is that it is introvert and specialised and lacks the impulse to attack large issues. But this state of affairs need not last forever and may even be an

interval of preparation in which poets forge new weapons before taking larger risks and regaining some of the territory which they have lost from being too particular about their aims.

That perception about the state of poetry is as relevant to writing in schools in the 1990s as it was to the general poetry scene in the 1960s.

Anthologies

It is at this point that we begin our 'descent' from the theoretical level of the consideration of the texts and contexts of poetry to the business of what goes on in the classroom. The first stage in this exploration will be to look at the particular context in which poetry finds itself in the classroom.

In its Autumn 1983 and Spring 1984 issues, *The Use of English* published articles by Nick Jones on the nature and use of poetry anthologies in secondary schools. The first one, 'On Anthologies', defined three 'orders' of anthology, and the second looked at the setting of poetry for examinations.

Apart from samplers, which Jones characterized as 'preliminary' to his three orders, there were 'first order' anthologies, like Alfred Alvarez's *The New Poetry* (1962), which tended to be composed by poets and which were almost always polemical in nature. Then came the 'second order', which consisted of selections with a longer perspective (for example, *The Faber Book of Modern Verse* (1982)). In these anthologies, the editor's role was largely judicial. Finally there was a 'third order' of anthologies which were 'distributive' in function. It was through these anthologies that the canon of 'English literature' was disseminated in schools.

The third order of anthology makes up the bulk of what appears on stockroom shelves – anthologies that are marketed for English departments. How are these anthologies structured, what are the values that underpin them and who are the poets that are making up the canon?

· In anthologies published since 1979 there are at least four principles of arrangement: by author, by theme, by poetic form and in arbitrary fashion (for example the alphabetical listing by title in *The Rattle Bag* (Heaney & Hughes 1982)) – the main pleasure of which is the unexpected contiguities between poems. This sequence of principles of arrangement might well represent an evolutionary development in the history of the school anthology. Chronological arrangements, it will be noticed, do not appear at all in this group of anthologies, and so the most 'primitive' structure – and by far the easiest to compose – is the one based on authors. Titles like *Nine Modern Poets* and *Ten Twentieth Century Poets* from the fifties and sixties had (and still have) a major influence on the way poetry is received by students, though most children I have worked with in schools seem healthily uninterested in the author of the poem they are reading. Of the anthologies surveyed in the present study, only *Meet and Write* (Brownjohn and Brownjohn 1985), *One World Poets* (Jones 1986) and *19th and 20th Century Verse* (Woodhead 1984) – the latter aimed at examination candidates – arrange themselves in this way.

By far the most popular means of arrangement is by theme. Often these themes are clearly stated in the contents lists: 'The World', 'Weather', 'The Night', 'Childhood', 'People', 'Old Age', 'Feelings' (!), 'Birds', 'Creatures' and 'Fantasy' from *Open the Door* (Greenwell & Peek 1984); 'Creatures' again, 'City', 'Country', 'People and Places', 'Dreams and Hauntings', 'War', 'School' and 'Religious Experience' from *Touchstones* (Benton & Benton 1987–8). In more offbeat and adventurous anthologies (often by poets), these archetypal and repeated themes are disguised in elliptical terms: 'First Day at School', 'He's Behind Yer', 'Tide and Time', 'Watchwords', 'Being-in-love', 'A Cat, A Horse and the Sun' and 'Smithereens' in *Strictly Private* (McGough 1981); 'Babes in Arms', 'At School Today', 'Wild Life' and 'Water, Water Everywhere' in *You'll Love This Stuff* (Styles 1986). Even when the themes are not stated, they are often subliminal.

Many children's experience of poetry in school, then, has been filtered through themes. I am concerned about this dependence on themes for two reasons. First, it seems that the themes chosen are almost always simple in nature. An individual poem is 'generalized' by being collected in this way, serving to illustrate some general truth rather than being read for its complexities. Second, one's attention is diverted from the text of the poem to what it is supposed to signify, and unless there is a return to the text one is likely to lose hold of the dynamic particularities of the poem.

Next in 'evolutionary' sequence is arrangement by formal features, by which I mean everything from the word level (assonance, alliteration etc.) through the line (rhythm, metre etc.) to the whole text. This is not new, of course, marking as it does a return to a rhetorical principle of arrangement, but it reflects a shift towards accounting for the shape of the text that is the concern of the present book. Examples of this kind of anthology are *The Kingfisher Book of Children's Poetry* (Rosen 1985) with 'Poems', 'Ballads', 'Limericks', 'Riddles in Rhyme' and 'Nonsense Verse' and in more modal style in *Poetry Horizons* (Andrews & Bentley 1987–8) which moves from 'Observing' through 'Telling' to 'Transforming' and 'Reflecting', and then in the second volume on to 'Imagery' and 'Political'.

In this and other anthologies, there is a distinct development within the collection from poems which build upon the report of the senses through narrative and other structures to the operation of the imagination and reflections upon experience. The political dimension – so often absent from such anthologies – is seen as a further extension of this line of development.

Another way of looking at anthologies published in the eighties is in terms of the poets they include.

About half the anthologies surveyed were devoted exclusively to twentieth century material. Most of the pre-twentieth century writers are from the established English canon, with the exception of Whitman, Dickinson and Longfellow. There is a distinct dearth of early writing from other cultures. Excluding specialist anthologies like *The Penguin Book of Women Poets* (Cosman *et al.* 1979) and the better collection from Bloodaxe (Couzyn 1985) – which by

Jones' definition, would be in the 'first-' or 'second-order' category – the best we can find as regards the representation of women is less than a third of the total, e.g. *Speaking to You* (Rosen and Jackson 1984) with 31%, *Into Poetry* (Andrews 1983) with 29% and *The Windmill Book of Poetry* (Orme 1987) and *I Like That Stuff* (Styles 1984) with 26% each.[1] All of these make a fairly wide international sweep, moving beyond the confines of the British canon.

An international spread of writers should at least be a consideration in the making of such anthologies, but many of them show little evidence of reading from beyond these or American shores. There are two excellent precedents in *New Ships* (Wilson 1975) and *Many People, Many Voices* (Hidden and Hollins 1978). The second of these and *One World Poets* (op. cit.) draw heavily on the Commonwealth tradition, whereas Morag Styles' collections are more eclectic, taking poems from Britain and Ireland, North America, Western Europe, Eastern Europe, Russia and Australasia.

Although *The Rattle Bag* has a smaller proportion of home-grown poems than many of the other anthologies (63%), the bulk of the rest is made up from North America (22%) and Eastern Europe (8%). There are good reasons for these preferences: both Heaney and Hughes have strong connections with American literature and Hughes in particular has worked on translations of East European writers – most notably in his founding of *Modern Poetry in Translation* with Daniel Weissbort. As poets, their own work has been informed by such influences.

Most striking of all is the extremely low proportion of works from Europe represented in these anthologies. In most cases, there is nothing. Only Morag Styles' anthologies, followed by the 4% of *The Kingfisher Book of Children's Poetry*, have substantial representations. 'Literature', in the sense of novels, plays and poems, has become less prominent in the syllabuses of modern European languages as the emphasis has moved to 'communicative' teaching methods, to speech rather than writing, to the wider world of texts. 'English' is becoming one of the places on the timetable when European literature might still find space.

Finally, we might expect the recommended lists of the five examining boards to alert teachers to the range of anthologies available, but only *The Rattle Bag*, the well-established *Touchstones* and *Strictly Private* appear, and these are all on the LEAG list (though the second of these appears on the NEA list). Most of the other recommendations are from the sixties and seventies. For all their faults, these 'third order' anthologies do aim to remake the world of poetry for their particular audiences. It is surprising how slowly the examining boards revise their lists, particularly when the lists of short stories, novels and plays do contain some more contemporary suggestions.

Workshops, manuals etc.

Since Nick Jones' article in the early eighties, there have been published several anthologies that do not come within his original taxonomy. Books like Sandy

Brownjohn's *Does it Have to Rhyme?* (1980) and *What Rhymes with 'Secret'?* (1982), Jill Pirrie's *On Common Ground* (1987), Mike Hayhoe and Stephen Parker's *Words Large as Apples* (1988), Jan Balaam and Brian Merrick's *Exploring Poetry 5–8* (n.d.) and Michael Rosen's *Did I Hear You Write?* (1989) could all be described as guides to writing poetry; they are rather like recipe books. They are characterized by the preponderance of prose expository text on the part of the author, interspersed with poems by children and established writers as illustrations of what can be done or as incentives and springboards. As books, they fall into a tradition exemplified by Ted Hughes' *Poetry in the Making* (1967) or Kenneth Koch's *Wishes, Lies and Dreams* (1970).

Although these titles all come under the broad heading of 'working anthologies', and although their aim is to encourage the writing of poetry, their approaches are very different. Each of them represents a distinctive viewpoint on the development of poetic writing in schools, and it is worth exploring their different viewpoints to see how they stand in relation to the creative writing movement discussed earlier in this book, and which pre-dated these approaches by about twenty years or so.

Poetry in the Making has been hugely influential but it is hard to apply its message in a school context. Essentially, its focus is on the nature of attention and on the development of the imagination. In this sense, it is firmly in the 'creative writing' mould, as is its assumption that 'the latent talent for self-expression in any child is immeasurable' (p. 12). Having said that, it is not of the 'stimulus' school: the poems included (mostly by Hughes, his contemporaries, a few Americans and Vasko Popa) 'are meant to serve as models for the kind of writing children can do without becoming false to themselves' (p. 12). Its format as a book derives from its origin as radio broadcasts in the *Listening and Writing* series: there are chapters on capturing animals, wind and weather, people, learning to think, and landscape as well as those based around two of Hughes' books for children, *Meet My Folks* and *Moon Creatures*. But although its structure is loosely thematic, its approach is imaginative. Having described his own start in writing poetry, Hughes asks how do you control words that 'are pouring out'? The answer is (p. 18):

> ... imagine what you are writing about. See it and live it. Do not think it up laboriously, as if you were working out mental arithmetic. Just look at it, touch it, smell it, listen to it, turn yourself into it. When you do this, the words look after themselves, like magic.

This involves, more than anything, an effort of concentration: 'The minute you flinch, and take your mind off this thing, and begin to look at the words and worry about them ... then your worry goes into them and they set about killing each other.' (ibid.)

Such writing, then, is not a product of the unconscious mind, but rather a product of the super-conscious mind; the writer is alert to the sensuous nature of experience through his or her imagination. The composing act is implicitly meditative. It becomes more explicitly meditative in 'Learning to Think' (especially on pp. 63–4) where Hughes suggests exercises in which children focus on objects for short periods, trying to capture the life and special qualities of the objects in words.

Hughes' note to teachers at the end of the initial section on 'Capturing Animals' fills out the methodology of this approach, and he describes it as 'headlong, concentrated improvisation on a set theme' (p. 23). The assumption is that the children are given the theme or subject by the teacher, even if that subject is given some time beforehand to allow the writers to carry it in their heads before they write. But when it comes to the writing itself, Hughes recommends that artificial limits of length ('say one side of a page') and time (a minimum of ten minutes) be imposed to bring about a crisis and so galvanize the mind into action; and that each phrase should be given a new line, so to create a free verse poem with its focus on meaning and expression, its life generated by the imagination. Later in the book, Hughes is more explicit about the function and nature of the imagination in children's writing (p. 51):

> All imaginative writing is to some extent the voice of what is neglected or forbidden, hence its connection with the past in a nostalgic vein and the future in a revolutionary vein. Hence, too, its connection with the old Adam, with volcanoes, world-endings, monstrous outrages etc.

The book most clearly in this tradition is *On Common Ground*; indeed, its foreword is by Ted Hughes. The qualities he picks out as the keys to Jill Pirrie's success as a teacher in getting marvellous poems from a large number of children are precision and honesty in observation, and giving to the pupils the confidence of their own impressions. One result of the first set of qualities is that the works created, even though they may be 'beautiful', have 'the air of being a by-product of a more serious purpose; the felicities of image, word and music, no matter how remarkable they may be, remain secondary and incidental' (p. x). In other words, the form these observations and imaginings take is of less importance that their content and purport, and the general effect on the class is to lift them to a

> special state of mind where new resources become accessible, and where their brains perform, quite naturally, feats of interconnection and perception which were previously unthinkable for them. (p. xi)

It seems to me to be a combination of these and other factors that bring about this 'special state of mind'. Pirrie's book, as well as drawing on the detailed and original observations of the children, aims for an easy interconnectedness between the voices of the children and the different voices of literary texts that come into the classroom like other people's voices. Sometimes these are used as models, and Pirrie is not afraid of the word 'exercise' to help elicit a richness of response, or at least to give the children a sense of the possibilities of expression. There are structures – ways of looking and telling – in existing poems which she draws on to help children make similar perceptions. But once used to gain a perspective, these structures can of course be left behind. Like the image in Heaney's poem 'Scaffolding',

> We may let the scaffolds fall
> Confident that we have built our wall.

There is no single strategy or approach taken: the thematic, the literary, the structural and the observational all lead to the same end: the enhancement of the imagination and the refining of the language.

Sandy Brownjohn's books are more singular than *On Common Ground* in that they concentrate on games and poetic forms rather than on observation and imagination. This narrower focus is different from that of the creative writing movement and the work of the Hughes-Pirrie tradition in a number of ways. It is aimed at teachers of children of roughly the same age-band (8–13) and is more oblique – but no less effective, if the children's poems are anything to go by – in its approach. The aim is not so much to reach states of concentration and perception as to *play* with language, and in particular with the structures of language as caught in literary and other texts; so the emphasis is on a different kind of concentration, which might be termed formal, mathematical and closed (as the rules of a game are closed) rather than openly scientific. As teaching techniques, these are more replicable and less dependent on the magical transformational power of a particular teacher; and yet they are more limited. They are likely to produce a degree of success for more children, but are less likely to uncover the originality in a smaller number.

One of the common elements between the two approaches is that the workshop activities were carried out with children between the ages of 9–13. In some ways, this might be a seen as a particularly 'poetic' phase in which most children have sufficient command of writing to be able to compose poems, and at which they also have an 'integrated' imagination: one in which, to adapt Yeats' phrase, blood, spirit and intellect run together. It is noticeable that in his foreword to *What Rhymes with 'Secret'?* and to *On Common Ground*, Hughes casts a cold eye on what happens to this burgeoning imagination at secondary school level. We will return to the question of the fall from grace in the practical chapters. My contention here is that the 'fall', such as it is, is partly a result of the perception that poetry inhabits an Eden-like zone: that it is somehow elevated above ordinary discourse and that it speaks a special language.

Two books that work at the outside edges of the 9–13 age range are *Exploring Poetry 5–8*, and *Words Large as Apples*, aimed at the 11–18 range. The introduction to *Exploring Poetry* seems to operate under the assumption of the pre-lapsarian myth (p. 1):

> The magic of poetry in the very early years is as strong as the magic of story; yet poetry seems to lose that power as children move into the upper years of the primary school.

But exactly the same has been argued at each stage of the education process, particularly at around 13. Nevertheless, the book aims to break down the barriers between poetry and other forms of discourse and activity by using drama, mime, painting and drawing, musical expression and the other arts to recreate the poem in question in different forms, or to extract elements of the poetic composition and use them as the basis of improvisation and further exploration. The emphasis throughout is on participation, the lifting of the text off the page and on engagement with the physicality of the poem – and thus on enjoyment.

While it is not the purpose of this book to focus on responding to poetry, it is clear that the activities suggested in *Exploring Poetry 5–8* form a foundation to the developing of response. But because response (reading) and production (writing) go hand in hand, each borrowing techniques and identities from the other, we can look at the work suggested for the 5–8 age range and see if there is any kind of continuous development through the middle years of education up to the 13–18 age range.

Would it be fair to say, for instance, if we were looking at the poetry curriculum from 5–18, that a movement from enactment through involvement, observation and imagination to increased awareness of the formal properties of poetry is a satisfactory model? Although such a model looks logical and elegant, and would seem to fit with Piagetian theories about development, I think we have to say that it is unsatisfactory as an indicator of development in poetry.

While Brownjohn's approach is formal in the sense that it works towards poetic expression through games, riddles, puns and other structures that are inherent in the everyday language occurring outside poetry, thus drawing on a rich vein in the language and mining it for poetic purposes, the work of Kenneth Koch, recorded in *Wishes, Lies and Dreams*, operates from a slightly different formal basis. Koch's work with 4th, 5th and 6th graders at Public School No. 61 in New York City in the late sixties is predicated upon a gamut of simple structural forms, not necessarily extracted from the living language but working as primal forms – even if fabricated – in the poetic mode. For example, one of Koch's most successful devices is the simple formula 'I seem to be . . ./But I really am . . .', giving rise to poems like:

I seem to be a bird careering around the sky
But really I am a leaf blown upon the wind.
I seem to be air, free to go where I like
But really I am earth, grounded and heavy.

Part of the structure is given, making it easy for children to pick up the phrase and develop it in their own way. Another example is a series of lines beginning with 'I wish . . .', either written individually or as a group or whole class. In both these examples, the primal or primitive form is repetition, and Koch uses this device repeatedly to get results. Comparison is also employed as one of the basic rhetorical devices of poetry, so that children can gain access to metaphors and similes quite effortlessly. According to Koch (p. 14),

> A poetry idea should be easy to understand, it should be immediately interesting, and it should bring something new into the children's poems. This could be new subject matter, new sense awareness, new experience of language or poetic form.

What is evident as we read Koch's account is that the writing produced rarely reaches beyond the structures that are employed to produce it. There is a similarity and limitedness about the poems, despite the encouragement to 'take risks'; sometimes the children seem forced to find feelings and experiences to fit their words, rather than the other way round. It seems as if some of the structures have too strong a hold on the imagination, which is forced to come up with alignments that are more fanciful than imaginative, and yet which do not carry the power of the surreal.

Part of the problem with this approach seems to be that the structures used are too small. There is little movement from the minimal starter structures like 'I wish . . .', 'I hear . . .' and so on to anything much larger or more expansive than the two-line structure of 'I seem to be . . ./But I really am . . .'. The result is that many of the poems are a collection of individual lines, with repetition of structures taking place every one or two lines, rather than anything more developed. In a sense, the products are Whitmanesque, on a much smaller scale.

Not all Koch's approaches are of this kind, however; the larger structures are reached, but by different and more conventional means: by playing music for the children to write to, by encouraging personification and writing in rôle, or by simply importing literary structures like pantoun or sestinas. Examples by children in these forms often show the strain of stretching beyond their natural voice(s). On the other hand, we have to weigh against this the exhilaration and sense of achievement of being able to write something that is recognizably poetry, which is close to the children's own preoccupations and language, and which gives the children a command of the basic forms of poetry.

So far we have mentioned three approaches to poetry: that of the 'creative writing' movement, captured and refined by Hughes and extended by Pirrie; that of the poetry-as-a-game school, represented by Brownjohn; and that of the 'primal structures' camp, as represented by the work of Koch. Another is the approach which introduces poems by established and non-established writers to act as 'models' – an approach used in some degree by all of those already mentioned; and yet another is the 'oral writing' approach, as described by Michael Rosen (1989) in *Did I Hear You Write?*

The 'literary model' approach is probably the most discredited of the five ways into poetry. It suffers this fate because it is associated with the 'old-fashioned' approach to the teaching of poetry: one that sees reading *per se* as the principal reason for encountering poetry, and which relegates the writing of poetry to a pleasant (or gruelling) exercise. In its crude form, this approach meant an apprenticeship to the classics, resulting in forced and often risible imitations of Keats, Shelley, Tennyson and other stalwarts of Palgrave's *Golden Treasury*, usually on set subjects and themes. Little must have been gained by this practice other than a working sense of how the poets built their lines, but many must have been lost to poetry through sheer boredom at the futility of the task. The 'creative writing' movement arrived like a bottle of Perrier to clear the stale alcoholic haze induced by this approach. But the stuffiness of the literary model approach ought not to prejudice us against its possibilities: given a wider range of models to imitate, and a less slavish attitude to the works of the past, imitation – as we know from classical precedents and from the work of Robert Lowell – can be enlightening as well as demanding. Indeed, opening up to the wide range of poetic forms that exists in world literature is a positive empowerment. The shift to imitation of *forms* rather than of style – a shift mirrored in literary theory and in the development of linguistics and stylistics in the 70s and 80s – and to an understanding of the contexts bearing upon those forms indicates the differences between this approach and its maligned precursor. Of all the approaches, it probably marries the study of literature and the practice of writing most closely. What it sacrifices is the imprint of personal 'voice', implying that such a voice is developed by attending to other voices and extending the range of one's own.

Needless to say, this approach has its detractors. Rosen (1989) attacks the excessively literary approach as promoting a view of language as outside and beyond the natural competence of most children. The Brownjohn books come in for criticism too, combining as they do this literary approach with one that is based on games and on playing with language; and the practices of using an object as stimulus (of running a poetry workshop like an art class) and placing the writing of poetry too close in time to the reading of it are questioned.

Rosen's viewpoint takes as its source and basis Auden and Garrett's formulation of poetry as 'memorable speech', and builds alongside its expression of remembered experience another dimension: that of imagined experience. It sees poetry as a way of preserving, reflecting upon and conversing about things, and is at pains to validate the oral mode rather than move too quickly to the written. What arises from this position – and from the practice informed by it – is 'oral writing', writing that remains close to the spoken voice and which invents forms. Rosen outlines several routes to oral writing, including storytelling, drama and the reading of poetry and urges the teacher to (p. 44):

> find forms that release children's knowledge, liberate it and so give the child a sense of his or her own power

rather than depend on conventional literary forms. One of the most useful aspects of *Did I Hear You Write?* is the appendix which contains an international range of books of and on poetry.

A recent publication stressing the importance of bilingual provision of poetry is by Raychaudhuri and Read (1990), *Bengali Poetry/English Poetry*. In the introduction, Sibani Raychaudhuri outlines the Bengali poetic; the similarities and differences with the prevailing British poetic are illuminating, as are the interactions between the two. For instance, poetry is the earliest form of literary activity in Bengali, and it was not until the nineteenth century that prose writing was introduced through English education. The most popular metre from the tenth to the nineteenth centuries was 'payar', a form in which each line consists of fourteen letters. Information like this helps to put the British poetic into perspective.

Poetry and the National Curriculum

In the first chapter of this book, we looked at the place of poetry in the National Curriculum, largely in terms of the problems in defining that place. Here, we look at the question again, turning our attention more to the practical possibilities of working with poetry in this framework, but finding it impossible to escape the problematic position that poetry has been put in.

The difficulty remains this: that although the proposals suggest that poetry is central to the concerns of English teachers, the very fact that the National Curriculum is assessment-driven, and the equally recognized fact that poetry is notoriously hard to assess, makes for an impasse. It 'must' be in the programmes of study for the three main profile components, speech and listening, reading and writing, and yet at the same time does not appear as a separate strand in the attainment targets.

Elsewhere in the report, however – largely in the recommendations for programmes of study – there are statements to the effect that pupils in key stage 2 (17.41(v)):

> should have plenty of opportunities to write poetry (whether individually, or in small groups, or as a class) and to experiment with different layouts, rhythms, verse structures, and with all kinds of sound effects and verbal play

or to write 'jingles, limericks, ballads, haiku etc.' (17.48 (iii)) or have the opportunity to select verse forms appropriate for their own choice of subject matter and purposes (17.54 (iii)).

It is ironic that in the programmes of study for reading, it is suggested that pupils' own writing should form part of the resources for reading. This is good and common practice, as is much else in this section of the report, but it sees the writing of poetry as subservient to the reading of it. Furthermore, many of the recommendations are conservative, like the learning of poems by heart, and the focus is predictably 'device' oriented (16.40 (iv)):

> Teachers should discuss a variety of works so as to bring out the range and effects of different types of sound patterning, e.g. alliteration, assonance, rhymes, onomato-poeia, and of figures of speech, e.g. similes, metaphors, personification.

As in the recommendations for the speaking and listening component, the emphasis is on reading aloud, on an international range of poems as well as on pre-twentieth century material, on performance, group and class discussion. One of the interesting and 'hidden' features of the proposals is the way poetry seems to get prominence in key stages 2 and 3, and then ceases to be mentioned, even as an example of a form of writing (except in the reading component) at the higher levels of attainment. It is as though poetry is associated especially with the 8–13 age group, as we have seen before.

What is heartening, however, is the understanding that practising the craft of writing poetry can lead to increased critical awareness of literary technique. And perhaps what is present by implication (to look generously at the recommendations and the subsequent orders) is that the practice of such craft will teach more *about language* than any amount of metalinguistic study.

Summary

This chapter has looked at various contexts in which poetry finds itself, particularly those educational contexts which bear directly on the place of poetry. The wider context of the British poetic was discussed first, and attitudes towards poetry arising from some of the historical factors had already been outlined in Chapter 3. Here, this poetic has been put in international perspective, and is seen to be only one of a number of possible ways to conceive the nature and function of poetry in a society.

The fact that most children's experience of poetry in schools is mediated through anthologies became the subject for exploration in the middle part of the chapter; this area of interest led in turn to a look at 'workshop anthologies' and at the various approaches – imaginative, literary, 'games-based' and via primal forms – to the teaching of poetry that they represent.

Finally, poetry has been viewed again in the light of the National Curriculum and found to be the object of reception by children (albeit in active ways) rather than something to be made.

It is at this point, having outlined the problems with poetry and having explored some of the reasons for these problems – in definition, in its relationship with 'ordinary' discourse, in accounting for its rhythms and in its wider contexts – that we can move on to try to solve some of these problems. What follows is one approach to the practicalities of handling poetry in the classroom. I have headed the chapters 'The oral dimension' and 'The visual dimension' in order to try and explore these two characteristics of the poetic message. These headings are but ways in to the solving of the problems of poetry. They overlap, and they are not exclusive. If there is an emphasis on form, it is to redress a balance, to make poetry as accessible to as many children as possible for as long as possible, and to build a bridge between oral and written forms. As Brian Powell (1968) suggested of his three interdependent elements basic to good writing – form, content and evaluation –

> this is the order in which they are of most help. The greatest need of the beginner is for guidance, not with what to say, but with how to say it. (p. 34)

Note

1 I have attempted to redress the balance in *Poetry* (Macmillan English Modules 1991).

6

The oral dimension

A pupil learns more about rhythm and cadence from writing five lines of verse, however poor, than scanning fifty.

J. L. Bradbury in *Journal of Education*, December 1932

In practice, what resources can we draw on as teachers to make poetry an accessible, exciting and powerful experience for children in schools? What approaches can we take to make the most of the encounters between children and poetic texts? This chapter focuses on the oral dimension to poetry, and the next on the written; together, they form the core of the practical section of this book and, along with the final chapter, aim to attempt to solve some of the problems with poetry that have been outlined and discussed in the first section.

Frye (1963) is surely right to see poetic rhythms as being as 'primary' as the associative rhythms of speech. Bouncing and clapping songs for babies establish the connection between movement, rhythm and words at the time of, or soon after, the dawning consciousness of meaning in the verbal interactions that take place from birth. Such songs and rhymes certainly predate the enjoyment of narrative in stories, and the ability to construct sentences. Nursery rhymes and songs, then playground chants, limericks and other such oral forms establish a large repertoire of poetic forms at a very early age. While all of these are poetic in form, the term 'poem' is rarely used to refer to them. They are part of the unconscious cultural patterning that in many ways sets the foundation for subsequent poetic development.

The other rhythmic strand that runs alongside the poetic is that of speech. Frye calls its rhythm 'associative'. It is not shaped by the repetitive rhythms of poetry, nor does it fall into the rhythmic unit of prose, the sentence. Instead, it works on the basis of the 'utterance'. There are plenty of points at which these associative rhythms begin to break into repetitive form, or indeed approximate and touch upon prose rhythms. It might be argued, for instance, that free verse, with its additive rhythms based upon the sense and rhythmic unit of the line, is closer in general to speech in this respect than metrical verse. But free verse is quite distinct in form and origin from nursery rhymes and bouncing songs.

There are thus as least two major sources of oral energy in poetry: that of the primary regular rhythms of songs and rhymes, and that of speech. But before we go on to see how these rich veins of poetic ore can inform and enliven poetry in the classroom, let us consider the connection between speech, voice and poetry again. In previous chapters, we have seen that some schools of thought and practice emphasize 'voice' as opposed to literary traditions; a dialectic is set up, its function to resurrect the claims of spoken culture, which it sees as having been suppressed by written culture and the cult of the 'text'. Such approaches often romanticize 'voice'; it becomes a metaphor, a banner under which to fight for the claims of the generalized voice of the oppressed. At a more literal, more practical and less ideological level, what are the qualities of voice that poetry draws on?

For a start, there is a poetry that is purely oral that operates in pre-literary cultures as well as in literary cultures, and a fascinating relationship between history, anthropology and childhood here, as we have already recognized that nursery rhymes and other forms popular in childhood belong to this category; there are people speaking, and as a transposition of that, creatures and things speaking too; there is a poetry which draws on the collaborative, interactive nature of speech; there is the semi-metaphorical notion of 'finding your voice', i.e. finding the particular rhythms and words to release some 'true' and fundamental self in verse; there is a poetry which speaks directly to a particular (or even a generalized, fictionalized) audience and which perhaps, like the work of Neruda or Brecht discussed in the last chapter, uses a different language to that of the more esoteric, indirect forms of poetry. In addition to these aspects of the relationship between poetry and speech, there are the processes and acts of writing which may, in various ways, move through speech in order to reach their final form – the question of drafting will be considered in this light. There are dialogic forms that can shape poems, oratorical influences and other more specific speech characteristics that have a bearing on the world of poetry: dialects, with their particular grammars, modulations and dictions; explorations in sound-poetry; and specific oral forms such as curses, charms, praises and spells.

Oral poetry

Most oral poetry collections exude the whiff of the primitive. An interesting point to consider in looking at these collections is the date at which the oral forms reached written form. Are these versions of oral discourse written down, or scripts for performance? If the former, are these malleable texts: what is their shape on the page? These collections draw heavily on the primitive because they associate speech with it, based on a projection from the fact that we learn to express ourselves in speech before we learn writing, and that the history of culture is one of speech followed by writing.

There are primal verse forms in these collections: listing is one device commonly used (see Barrs 1987), as in these lines from a Malaysian poem:

Wind would tear a dead man's shroud
Wind as sharp as edge of spade
Wind as keen as tip of axe

Not only is this a simple and effective way of organizing what you want to say, but it closely accords with the principle of the line that we have established as being central to poetry: a new line is started for each item on the list, and the 'entry' can be as long or short as you like. We can use this principle of listing to build a series of sessions on poetry. Either the Malaysian poem can act as a model (a more exciting one than the conventional 'Red is . . .' followed by a list of things associated with the colour red), or we can start by asking children to write down a list of pleasures (see Brecht's poem 'Pleasures' in Brecht 1976) or beautiful things or horrors or whatever. Each item on the list can then be 'expanded' to a few words or a much longer line. Here is an example of that development in the work of primary school children from London:

Pleasures	Horrible things
McDonalds	A dog
Seaside	mud
Holidays	flies
School	rats
Dogs	eggs
Cats	
The last look out of the window at night	
Television	
Friends	
Parents	

These simple and generalized lists were developed by the children in the following ways:

Pleasures

When you're at McDonalds,
it's so lovely you don't want to go home.
Seaside. Feeling the cold
sloshing water on your body.
On your holidays,
forgetting about everything else.
In school waiting to go home.
Dogs. Seeing them in shop windows.
Are you tempted?
                              (Mary Keegan)

Horrible things

The rustling of pigs in mud.
Dogs eating the rats.
The eggs getting old and bad.
Rats running round the house,
looking for food.
                              (Martin Keegan)

One child, Keith Vyas, chose to develop only three items from his initial list of eight 'scarey things', but his variation of line-length (even though there is a rawness about the handling of the conventions of starting new lines) is striking:

> The night is black with nothing to see except one thing
>   which is the silver ball moon.
> Spiders.
> The eight-legged web monster
>   that climbs in unexpected times.
> Lions with their vicious bravery,
> Their teeth sharp as needles.

These examples may seem too wooden, too bound by the lines which they have created; they seem manufactured and forced, perhaps. I would argue that writers like Vincent Lee, in the following poem which began as a list, may not have reached this position without some scaffolding to help him. Once the poem begins to take on a life and shape of its own, the scaffolding can fall away:

> The horizon
> almost
> sticking to the opposite.
> The apples dropping
> from a contrast of colours
> in the tree.
> Butterflies
> floating in the air.
> Flowers
> exploding rapidly. Fairies
> granting wishes.
> The sunlight drifting everywhere . . .

or, from another school, Carmel Christian's 'Things that remind me of summer':

> All the people on the sands sunbathing and such;
> cruising in the Caribbean;
> exotic food and moonlight romance.
>
> Ice cream cold with raspberry juice on a hot summer's day;
> swimming outside in an open air pool
> with the hot sun beating on your back;
> butterflies dancing on flowers
>   in the morning dew.
>
> A day outing to Ilkley;
> untouched scenery,
> with wild heather growing
>   like a purple curtain.

It is evident in Carmel's poem that the list format has been used to get the poem going, and has established an additive rhythm, but that this mould is broken in interesting ways: first, by the breaking of the poem into stanzas (of three, five and four lines respectively); second, by the breaking of a long unpunctuated line ('swimming outside in an open air pool with the hot sun beating on your back') into two separate lines; third, by indentation at the end of the second and third stanzas. In the case of the last line of the poem, the indentation is coupled with the first and only simile of the poem to give the poem an added – and distinctive – sense of closure. There seems no sense in which the writer has been inhibited by the form.

Another development of the list is in poems of the kind championed by Kenneth Koch, in which an opening phrase is repeated, acting as a trigger to each line, section or stanza of the poem:

I can't stand the way spaghetti slides around
I can't stand the mould on jam when it has been left in the larder too long

I can't stand the smugness on people's faces when they think they know something
    and you don't, and they have to hold it over you like a carrot

These can be quite effective, especially if the trigger phrase is left behind as more expansive rhythms take over and the poem gains a momentum of its own, often driven by strong passion. Other such ideas for starting poems are 'Look at the way they . . .', 'I can remember . . .', 'Why did I . . . ?' or a phrase that will suggest a setting, like 'On a cold, bleak night . . .' or 'Invisible, in full sunlight . . .'. Judith Nicholls in *Magic Mirror* (1985) has a poem based on this principle called 'Night', which starts:

There's a dark, dark wood
inside my head
where the night owl cries . . .

and it is easy to move on to poems from an acknowledged literary tradition like John Clare's 'Pleasant Places':

Old stonepits with veined ivy overhung
Wild crooked brooks oer which is rudely flung
A rail and plank that beds beneath the tread
Old narrow lanes where trees meet over head
Path stiles on which a steeple we espy
Peeping and stretching in the distant sky
And heaths oerspread with furze blooms sunny shine
Where wonder pauses to exclaim 'divine'
Old ponds dim shadowed with a broken tree . . .

Furthermore, the list can be disguised within the poem, particularly within the 'descriptive' poem. Sukhbir's 'Still Life' has this quality:

On the roadside
a basket of vegetables
overfull

Two gourds, necks raised high
tender downy bodies
raw-green

as does, even more subliminally, Neruda's 'Oda al Tomate' ('Ode to the Tomato'), which starts:

La calle
se llenó de tomatoes,
mediodía,
verano,
la luz
se parte
en dos
mitades
de tomate,
corre
por las calles
el jugo.

('The street's
crowded with tomatoes:
midday,
summer,
light
falls
in two
halves
of a tomato,
and the juice
runs
through the streets.')

So it is that a simple seed – a single word in a list – can grow and transform itself into a recognizably complex poem. The movement is also from speech structures to written structures (and the text will be returned to speech in a reading). The list is not an exclusively oral structure, of course; it finds more literary form in, for example, the entries in *The Pillow Book of Sei Shonagon* (1971), a journal kept by a tenth century Japanese courtesan, under headings like 'Embarrassing things', 'Things that make one's heart beat faster', 'Things that cannot be compared', 'Things that arouse a fond memory of the past', 'Things that give a clean feeling' and 'Things that have lost their power'. Here is part of an entry entitled 'Surprising and distressing things':

All night long one has been waiting for a man who one thought was sure to arrive. At dawn, just when one has forgotten about him for a moment and dozed off, a crow caws loudly. One wakes up with a start and sees that it is daytime – most astonishing.

One of the bowmen in an archery contest stands trembling for a long time before shooting; when finally he does release his arrow, it goes in the wrong direction.

These items in the lists can also be as short as one word. The principle of free verse that we explored in Chapter 4, with the variations of long lines and short, is seen at work in these entries.

Another principle at work in oral poetry – largely because memory has to be supported as you listen to the performance – is the narrative principle. The world's longest poems are narrative (e.g. the Kirghiz folk epic *Manas*, running to half a million lines, and classical epics like the *Odyssey* and *Iliad*). Perhaps the form that is best known in this field is the ballad, a form with a strong and unbroken (if not always fully acknowledged) place in British and North American oral and literary culture. We find the same sort of split between the oral tradition and the literary tradition in attitudes toward the ballad as we described earlier in relation to 'voice': the ballad has been undervalued because it has been seen as a 'folk' form, a subversive, often political, vehicle. De Sola Pinto and Rodway (1957), in their introduction to *The Common Muse*, attribute this perception to nineteenth-century critics influenced by Romantic medievalism: the medieval ballad was seen as a safe 'folk' product and eulogized as such, but the common street ballad was reviled for its 'unpoetic', contemporary rawness. But as the editors point out in their introduction, commerce between the rough-and-ready street morality of the broadside ballads on the one hand, and the more consciously crafted and refined literary ballads on the other, has usually been strong, to the benefit of both. They refer to Ralegh's reply to Marlowe's 'Come live with me and be my love' (both printed at one point as a single broadside sheet) as being more streetwise; these poems have been imitated and parodied by school children in this century:

> Come live with me and be my love!
> Not in a mansion but the flat above.
> It's not very big, but grand enough
> For you and me and all our stuff.
> (Lisa Salsbury)

as well as by C. Day Lewis, very much in the tradition of the street ballad with its wordly, comic, often political nature as opposed to the more refined, distant and less contextualized romantic ballad. So while the ballad form can hardly be called 'primitive', it is typical of the oral (often sung) forms that constitute narrative verse.

There is more than one way to tell a story, though, and narrative structures appear in many other different forms in poetry. Usually the line is longer than in the lyric, in order to accommodate the material, and the poem longer, too. Whereas the ballad is almost always rhymed ABAB and couched in 'ballad metre', other narrative poems tend to blank verse rather than free verse. Blank verse of pentameter or larger scale gives momentum as well as space; perhaps Wordsworth's 'Michael' is a good example of such a poem, but shorter and less metrical stories are told by Nakasuk and Taufiq Rafat, for example (both collected in Andrews 1983), and provide more accessible models for children to work with:

> There is a tribe of invisible men
> who move around us like shadows – have you felt them?

begins the Nakasuk poem, which then moves into the story itself with

> It once happened that a human woman
> married one of the invisible men . . .

The Rafat poem begins:

> When the telegram arrived
> I was combing my hair in the sun
> And gossiping with the servants.

It is as though the shorter narrative scope of these two poems needs less of the supporting structure of regular metre, let alone rhyme. There are more primitive narrative structures, though, for example in creation myths which often take the form of an imaginative and logical sequence of happenings:

> In the beginning was space
> which gave birth to more space.
> Between the two spaces was a line,
> ever-changing, sometimes disappearing
> as the two spaces merged, but
> forming again as they moved apart.
> Then came a song,
> then words,
> which begat pain
> which begat hardship
> which begat clouds
> which begat rain
> from which the seas formed, slowly.
> Then life amongst the rock pools.

These can vary from strictly repeated and modulated sequences, many of which Ted Hughes used in his quasi-mythological *Crow*, to long, flowing stories. It is possible also to move away from mythological stories to a retelling of folk tales, using various devices of print in order to catch the drama of the voice as well as to suggest the performance of the poem:

> OFF
> they went
> The hare speedily, hastily, quickly, whisked past
> the tortoise.
> The tortoise small, short,
> and bulky,
> followed

> slowly,
>   lumbering,
>   and slugging
> behind . . .
>
> (Janie Lai)

and then further to move into the framing of anecdotes in verse, the telling of life stories or 'life-in-the-day' tales, as well as to use a reflective, meditative narrative approach. Experimentation in the telling of a story is one of the possibilities that poetry offers, particularly when the layout of the words on the page tries in some way to represent the content of the poem. It is liberating to realize that poetry, with its line by line approach, is another way of telling, and that one does not have to be confined by the sentence-bound nature of prose, or by its expected length.

Lyrics

It is perhaps surprising that although songs are an essential part of many children's lives – from nursery rhymes to pop, folk, rock and jazz lyrics – the lyrics of these songs have not been seen as a resource to draw on in the exploration of poetry. Lyric poetry, or poetry 'sung to the lyre' was a staple in classical Greek culture, and it was the words which were of primary importance. Its various forms, like dirges, wedding-songs and procession-songs (prosodion) had distinct social and ritualistic functions (see Howatson 1989). But the movement of poem away from song, partly owing to the canonization of the poem as literature, has made this connection more tenuous. The problem remains that adolescents, in particular, see little connection between the songs they sing to themselves on the one hand, and poetry on the other. Attempts to make a connection often fail if the teacher imports his or her current passion to the classroom. Similarly, any recommendation made here will quickly go out of date. The key is to put the children in the position of experts, asking them to make a small anthology of lyrics that they like, and to put these lyrics alongside poems. Differences and similarities can then be judged; readings of the lyrics and poems recorded alongside the sung versions; and, if possible, different versions of the same lyric collected. Displays of record sleeves, posters, sheet music and books of lyrics can be organized, and collaborations with the music and art departments undertaken.

Everyone, everything speaking

Speech in most cases is improvisatory, interactive, associative and informal. Poetry that draws on this fund of associative rhythms and expressions can take on some of these qualities; if well-crafted, the poetry will hang between the casual style of speech and the more formal qualities of written discourse and generate an exquisite tension and electricity. Sometimes you don't have to do much to move speech into a poetic frame. Here is Dolores Dante talking about her life as a waitress in the USA in Studs Terkel's *Working* (1977):

I have to be a waitress.
How else can I learn about people?
How else does the world come to me?
I can't go to everyone.
So they have to come to me.

Everyone wants to eat,
everyone has hunger.
And I serve them.

The rhetorical shaping in

Everyone wants to eat
everyone has hunger

(a kind of shaping that is used many times in her account of her work) is not the sole province of poetry, but it works here as well as it works in ordinary speech or in oratory. Dolores Dante is talking about her own life; it is possible for us also to talk about our own lives in this way, but it is further possible to talk as if we were someone or something else. When 'speaking as yourself' can be inhibiting (partly, I suspect, because all of us are a blend of separate selves and feel confused when asked to tell our single 'true' self), speaking and writing in role can, paradoxically, reveal more of our own selves than of the role we are taking on; there is often an increase in power and 'sincerity' in the voice. Many established poets, like Pound, Yeats, Keats and Browning have found that writing in other voices has enabled them to develop a surer sense of their own voice.

There is a Mongolian oral form called 'The word of . . .'. It is used to express the 'word' of an animal, and can be used as an introduction to in-rôle writing. It is a blank verse form, so the monologue can develop to whatever length seems appropriate:

The 'word' of a watch-dog

He who is my master
Fondly brought me up
From my earliest years
To splendid maturity,
And put me in charge
Of all that he owns.
When a stranger approaches
I go to meet him from afar.
Furiously I threaten him
And try to drive him off . . .

This activity is given an extra magic if it is introduced by the Eskimo poem 'Magic Words' (collected in Rothenburg 1972), which begins:

In the very earliest time
when both people and animals lived on earth,
a person could become an animal if he wanted to
and an animal could become a human being . . .

Like any of the in-rôle poems, the content can be freely imagined or be the result of research and/or observation. The following poem was written after a visit to a chocolate factory:

Boredom

Blick
My day has started
I walk and walk
along the never ending corridors
Left and right turns
Here and there
Up some stairs
And through a door
The noise hits me
Like a bang on the head
I nod to my friends
And they smile back
No use talking, you see
I walk quickly to my place
And sit down on the chair
Still warm from the last shift
I begin my same old job
Filling up tubes
The ones the machine has missed
For several hours I sit here
Then someone taps me on the shoulder
He points to the clock on the wall
Time to go
Doors, corridors, stairs
Again
The end of another day
Blick

(Rachel Allen)

and a historical dimension can be built in to such poems. Inanimate objects and concepts can be given voices too, and give rise to substantial monologues. In-rôle writing of this kind can, of course, take prosaic or dramatic form too; there is no prescription to adopt poetic shape. But the distinctively associative and often fragmentary nature of the speaking voice can often find a satisfactory home in the line-based and apparently improvisatory rhythms of poetry.

Riddles are one form in which creatures and objects are given voices, and in which the game of disguising the identity of the subject within metaphor is played with delicate energy. They can range from one-liners through short poems to texts extending to the lengths of dramatic monologues; from this Yugoslavian riddle from Vasko Popa's collection *The Golden Apple* (1980):

I'm darkest when it's light; I'm hottest when it's cold; I'm coldest when it's warm.
(Answer: cellar.)

through this longer one from the same collection:

I am young and slender.
When I travel I have a tail.
The further I go
The less there is of my tail.
I lose it as I go
And come home tailless.
(Answer: needle and thread.)

to this poem by Ai Qing, in which the riddle-pattern is clearly distinguishable, but
in which the poetic form is equally clearly established:

Though just a plain surface,
Yet it seems unfathomable.

It loves truth deeply,
Never hiding defects.

It is honest with those who seek it,
Anyone can discover himself in it,

Whether one is flushed with wine
Or wears hair as white as snow.

Some like it
Because they are good-looking.

Some avoid it
Because it is too frank.

There are even some
Who hate it and wish to smash it.

as it is in Sylvia Plath's more well-known poem of the same name, 'Mirror'.
Children delight in the writing of such riddle-poems, and in guessing each
other's subjects:

I can be big and small.
I can rise or fall.
You can blow me up,
You can let me down.
I can blow in the wind.
I can bring happiness and play –
tie a knot,
get the string,
let me float in the wind.
When I am here, it is playtime.
Blowing me up is not a crime.
                              (Thomas O'pray)

Each of these riddle poems is metaphorical in nature: they transform one thing into another. That same principle is at work in Geoffrey Holloway's poem 'Band Call' (in Middleton 1989) in an eminently accessible way:

Horn   You are a snarly broth and breath of a lion
         with its eye-teeth in the sun's shoulder,
         cut loose, riding its golden high;
         the loping off in a cool pride
         of violence deferred.

Drums You are woodpeckers drilling a dream forest,
         a million reindeer running with the wind,
         a rogue elephant crashing through leaves of moonlight . . .

and in another way, in more extended form, in Rabindranath Tagore's 'Palm-tree.'

Collaborative poems

Poems do not have to be written by individuals. One way to break the ice at a poetry writing session is to set up collaborations in which a group can create a poem. A simple way to effect this is to suggest a common theme, like 'Earliest memories' or 'Childhood fears'; or to supply a trigger phrase, like 'I want to be . . .' or 'If only . . .'. The class can be divided into groups or four or five, then each individual in the group writes a single line based on the theme or refrain. When the lines, which can be of any length, have been written, they are placed together and the group decides which order will suit them best. The completed stanzas are then read out by one member of each group to make up the whole 'class poem', and it may well be that after this first complete reading, the class will decide that the order of the stanzas needs to be changed. Such an exercise can produce not only a sense of satisfaction, but will avoid the embarrassment of a first exposure of one's poetry to an audience and may generate some fine writing. An alternative to this approach is to send pupils off for fifteen minutes or so on their own to observe and make notes on the school or any other common environment; they return into small groups to pool their observations, add others, and arrange the various contributions into a satisfying whole.

Another approach is described by Pam McEwen (1989). With a Super Bowl football game coming up, she had her children brainstorm words, phrases, ideas and feelings which she jotted down on a large sheet of paper. Acting as scribe, she wrote down as the children composed. They moved on from there (p. 552):

suggesting, refining, adding, deleting, and rereading it at least 100 times until at the end they knew it by heart.

The final version – the result of 'brainstorming, rehearsing, choral reading, assisted reading, memorizing, sequencing and vocabulary development' read:

Super Bowl XXII

With pigskin in hand
John Elway spirals

the bomb to Steve.
The crowd goes wild –
confetti flies out of the stands
and streamers bounce and float
onto the field.
Steve scrambles to the fifty-yard line,
he stumbles,
but wait –
he's up,
he's hugging the ball
under one arm.
A ferocious beast-like Redskin
slams into his side;
he's knocked off guard
but recovers
and sprints to the end zone.
TOUCHDOWN!
The crowd is on its feet
cheering, yelling, screaming
GO BRONCOS!!

Poems that take on more than one voice can be written in rôle, thus combining the in-rôle approach described above with the notion of collaboration. One of the most accessible and successful forms for developing this is a double monologue (it can hardly be called a dialogue) between two young people, as in this poem by Parisjat Banomyong:

She: When we met I knew it was love at
      first sight for him.
      He kept trying to chat me up,
      and he even followed me home.
      I finally (after much persuasion) agreed to
      go out with him on Friday.
      He seemed quite nice.

He: When we met I knew it was love at
      first sight for her.
      She was practically following me,
      asking what I was doing on Friday.
      I finally gave in (I felt so sorry for her).
      She seemed quite nice.

This can be written by one hand, of course. Its strength is in the irony of its mutually incompatible viewpoints. The poem could either be continued with these two characters along these lines, or used as a model for double monologues (or genuine dialogues) between lovers, defendants and prosecutors in court, parents and children and other pairs of characters.

Related to this approach, but taking different shape, is the pattern of question-and-answer. One of the most generative poems in this mould is 'Dream of a

Bird', by Bach Nga Thi Tran (in Heylen and Jellett 1987) in which questions are asked of each statement that a person makes about her dreams. The effect of a question following each statement is to urge the imagination to make a further step in the exploration of feelings, so that before long a simple beginning like 'I dreamt I was a bird' is transformed into a revealing and engaging insight into the motivation for the dream. Again, because the poem is built up line by line by two hands, there is little sense of incapability in the writers; before they know where they are, they have created a poem, and usually a poem of telling and original power. Whether the development of the poem is comic, absurd, surrealist, sad, political and/or personal, there is always a strong line of development, and so an imaginative logic is established. Here is an example of how such a poem could begin:

I found myself on a pier, amongst the amusements.
Why were you there?
I was dawdling, passing the time between school and home.
But why there?
It was somewhere I'd loved as a child. I used to come here with my mum and dad
    on a Sunday; we'd spend hours on the pier.
Why did you love it?
The lights, the crazy sounds of the machines . . .
Why did the lights attract you?
At home things were never that bright.
Why?

And so on. One of the interesting questions arising from working like this is when to stop. The question-and-answer structure invites a continuous backwards and forwards motion in the poem and in itself, to borrow Smith's (1968) terminology, suggests no obvious means of closure (except perhaps a shorter – or longer – last line or a ceasing of the questions). But closure is usually not a problem. Thematically, these poems tend to move toward a revelation or other climax of some kind, and then to end in a brief coda. They are like dramatic narratives, prompted and shaped by the questions.

It might be argued that structural scaffolds like these are anathema to the proper development of writing, and especially to the writing of poetry which should be 'free of structural inhibition, totally expressive and organic in form'. I have suggested earlier in the book, in the more theoretical chapters, that it is naive to think that we are ever entirely free of structure and form when we compose. We are free to choose our route through the generic landscape, and are free in our ability to express whatever we like, but those freedoms are often aided rather than cramped by formal structures. In the clogged and difficult-to-navigate waters of the river of expression, it can be helpful to be offered structures that ease the passage to more complex and more sensitive forms of discourse rather than to be given no help at all. These approaches are by no means a panacea for poetry; they do not solve all the problems that many children and adults have in encountering it; they are simply one way of trying to give more people access to a powerful mode of discourse. Cromley (1976) describes her work with 'remedial readers' (and writers), where the structures offered are far more prescriptive and full than in any other work presented in this book. She calls these 'skeletal poems', and they almost look like cloze exercises – except of course that the material supplied by the writer is personal and affective. Here is an example:

> Who am I?
> My parents think I'm . . . .
> My friends think I'm . . . .
> And I know that I'm . . . .
>
> Sometimes I'm . . . .
> Other times I'm . . . .
> Most of the time I'm . . . .

While this looks at first sight both dull and prescriptive, at least it would offer a poor writer/reader the chance to complete a full (poetic) text, even if the scaffolding or skeleton takes up the major part of the construction. We can envisage a progression from this heavily supported writing through various stages to a more independent position.

As with other (oral) forms that we have been considering, it is possible to start with primitive and simple question-and-answer structures (as in 'Dream of a Bird', Miroslav Holub's 'Conversation with a Poet' in *On the Contrary* (1984) or Ted Hughes' 'Examination at the Womb Door' in *Crow* (1970)), and move to more complex and more embedded versions of those structures. A single-line question followed by a single-line answer can be developed in various ways. One is to assign the question to the title of the poem, or to begin a poem with a question, like Keats' sonnet 'Why did I laugh tonight?'. Another is to end a poem with a question or questions, usually representing unresolved situations and/or feelings and genuine requests for further enlightenment. Some poems – like some shorts by Carl Sandburg – consist of nothing but questions; others are like riddles. The result is to expose the dialectical nature of much supposedly univocal lyric verse. One could argue that even without question-marks, many poems are in effect answers to questions, or at least part of a rhetorical dialogue. There are further examples of question-and-answer poems in an article by Raymond Wilson (1982), 'Did you ever see a poet?' in which the initial questions – like 'Did you ever see a pigeon?' or 'Did you ever see my gran?' – are followed by compound epithets, Dylan Thomas-style:

> Did you ever see a crane-fly?
> Lanky-legged, wispy-winged, proudly-prancing, fragile.

Another form of collaboration is the renga, or 'chain of poems'. Rather like a game of consequences, one writer begins a poem in a particular form, and the next writer takes up the thread and develops the poem. In the Japanese tradition in which the renga originates, there were strict rules about the nature of the form and the transitions: unequal sections of three lines (of 5, 7 and 5 syllables, as in haiku) and two lines (both of seven syllables) are prepared by two poets and then linked. The rules for multiplication from then on are complex, but poems were supposed to move through five phases of development: *hen, jo, dai, kyoku, ryu* (start, prelude, theme, centre, fall). These rules can be interpreted freely or ignored for the purposes of writing in schools: pupils can either write as little as a line each, or compose couplets, tercets or quatrains, or vary their contributions as the spirit takes them. They may write in pairs, alternating voices; or write in groups of increasing size, making the 'chain' longer.

There is an international collection of renga, written collaboratively by Octavio Paz, Jacques Roubaud, Edoardo Sanguineti and Charles Tomlinson and published by Penguin (Paz *et al.* 1979) which will give a much fuller account of the form. One feature worth mentioning here is the emphasis on exploring the truth collaboratively rather than individually; of looking for meaning in translation and correspondence rather than in individual soul- or self-searching. It is a different poetic to the conventional one, and one very much in accord with the argument of this book: its focus firmly on the concert of voices rather than on the expression of a single voice.

Another form of collaboration is that between writer and editor. We will turn to this relationship in a separate sub-section.

Drafting and editing poetry

I include a section on the drafting and editing of poetry in this chapter for a number of reasons. The principal one is that the emergence of the final version of a poem from a draft or (more usually) a series of drafts is often seen as an evolution of polished and refined print from rough and ready voice. Even though the actual movement of the revisions might be from a literary frisson to a more 'natural' speaking voice style, the overriding sense of development is from utterance to text. This direction is confirmed by reports from writers of the first stirrings of poems coming as rhythmic phrases of inner speech (e.g. Middleton 1973 quoted on p. 130), often expressed in musical terms. But part of my purpose here is to test whether indeed that is the general direction of the creative impulse, and as an application of these findings, whether drafting and editing can help or hinder the emergence of the 'final' text.

Drafting would seem to have a good deal to offer to poetry, more because of the nature of poetry than that of drafting. First, as is immediately obvious, most poems are relatively short. That means that if we are to consider rewriting the whole text, the task is not as burdensome as it might be if we were writing a novel, or even a short story. Second, the freedom from formal constraints that early drafts allow, make for an access to relatively un- or sub-conscious levels of writing impulse (sometimes called 'creative' impulses), the energies of which poems in particular tend to draw on. Third, the simultaneous drive towards precision in form and expression, in free verse as well as in more regularly rhythmic verse forms, is given the opportunity to do its work.

Let us consider some drafts to see if these possibilities are realized. These are some observations I made and noted down while looking from the window of our house in York, several years ago. They are snapshots, as if I had taken them with an instamatic camera, of a man and his dog:

> His grey hair – blowing over his eyes –
> untidy – he stops to read the evening paper
> while his dog pees in the gutter
>
> He's moving along slowly now
> – shuffling.
> His alsatian is anxious to move on.
>
> Suddenly he comes to and sets off
>   at a faster than usual pace.

Already the writing is suggesting a form; without my deciding anything, it seems to be falling roughly into three-line sections, as if the length of each perception, or a rhythm driving them, was fairly constant. Furthermore, all but one of the eight lines are of roughly the same length. There's a dissatisfaction with the writing, too. If not, I would have left it as it stands. The dissatisfaction stems more from the lack of specificity than from an unhappiness with the form and shape of the text.

On to the second draft (see Fig. 1): note that even at this stage, the punctuation is loose. There are a few full stops, but otherwise the emergent text is divided by dashes which separate one perception from another. To use Frye's categories again, this is associative and speech-like rather than poetic. Almost all the changes have the effect of increasing the precision with which we see the man: he is a particular man in a particular place, rather than anyone. Two of the three emergent stanzas have been deleted: in the final version which includes three further stanzas that have emerged alongside the first two, you will see that they have been combined.

> His grey uncut hair blowing over his eyes
> he stops to read *The Evening Press*
> while his alsatian pees in the gutter.
>
> He's shuffling along now, still reading,
> on the end of the dog's lead.
> Suddenly he's yanked forward towards a lamp-post.
>
> So he pulls hard on the lead
> which tightens round the dog's neck
> and the dog stops dead.
>
> Now I can see his double-crossed eyes,
> his heavily-lined skin wrinkling like a prune;
> his bad teeth, his unshaven chin.
>
> The dog is angry, resentful.
> He hits it. It snarls back,
> then follows after in his tired slippers.

                    uncut
His grey/hair - blowing over his eyes -
                               Press
~~untidy~~ - he stops to read ~~the~~ The ~~Evening~~ Evening paper

while his ~~dog~~ dog pees in the gutter.
         alsatian

                                              still reading
~~He's moving along slowly now~~ He's shuffling along now/
~~- shuffling.~~   on the end of the ~~dog's~~ dog's lead

~~His alsatian is anxious to move on.~~

                  he's yanked forward
Suddenly ~~he comes to and sets off~~

~~at a faster than usual pace.~~

   and pulled along towards a lamppost
   so he pulls hard on the lead
   which tightens round the dog's neck
       and the dog stops.

Now
~~When he looks up~~ I can see that his

eyes ~~are~~ double-crossed eyes,
                              wrinkles
His skin is (heavily-lined), like a prune
He has bad teeth; grey stubble on
     his chin and neck.

                ~~ill kept big powerful vicious~~
The dog is smouldering, resentful.
He hits it. It snarls back.
Then follows after his tired slippers.
The man is wearing an old coat -
ex-~~army~~ - and slippers.

Figure 1

The three-line stanza (tercet) is now established as the shape the poem is taking. The decision to regularize the shape in this way – which has evolved 'organically' from the original perceptions and notes – has meant that other stray phrases have been brought into line and, as noted above, two sections have been combined into one. The effect of the revisions in the evolution of this poem has been largely to refine existing material and to confirm an emergent shape; though the imaginative reflection upon the scene, once the immediate recording of it had passed, has the effect of filling out the picture and making it more specific and more life-like.

Not all drafts and revisions work in the same way. The poem by Vincent Lee, quoted earlier, had its first draft (after the simple list) in this form:

> The horizon allmost
> sticking to the opozit.
> The apples droping from
> a contrarst tree.
> Butterflies floating in
> the air. Flowers exploding
> raggedly. Fairies granting
> wishes. The sunlight
> drifting everywhere.
> Make up spread on people's
> faces. Drips and drops
> falling from old taps.

This looks like a poem already, but it represents a half-way house between prose and poetry for Vincent. It covered one page of his notebook, is marked by strongly defined sentences (and no other punctuation) and its layout is arbitrary. The move from this via slashes to mark the line-endings he wanted to the new layout of the poem (p. 80) is the crucial move towards poetic form, and it is one we have discussed earlier regarding the differences between poetry and prose. As well as that, there is the improvement in spelling, which is not relevant to our argument here.

The question of teacher intervention arises here. Given this draft by Vincent, what approach would we take as teachers to this emergent text? Are we simply going to leave it to him to decide the fate of the text, e.g. whether he will leave it as 'finished' in this current draft, or whether he will go on to revise further? Are we forcing him to adopt a particular poetic convention by asking him to 'break it into lines'? Do we 'suggest' or ask questions of him? These are all questions of pedagogical approach and are as pertinent to any form of writing or composition as they are to the poem, but nevertheless, the decisions taken will have a marked effect on the outcome of the poem. One central question is this: will Vincent gain more from working towards a polished, recognizably 'finished' poem, or will he gain more by working out formal questions for himself?

These are delicate questions, and it is probably fairly evident what we should *not* do. We should not be marking in the line-breaks and forcing the text into a poem on behalf of the writer: that may seem as arbitrary as having any line-ending and cannot give the writer much sense of the principles informing line-breaks in poetry. One solution here would be to give Vincent a much larger piece of paper – possibly without lines – so that he can arrange the text he has created on it according to principles that he will discover for himself. This could be effected by having him cut up the text into its individual words, and then experimenting with these until the best arrangement is found.

Another problem often faced by teachers is how to enable children to cope with forced rhyme. Here is part of a poem written by a Year 7 pupil which has real momentum, and yet which seems confined by its (almost) relentless rhyme pattern:

A Snorkle of a Holiday

The sea is calm and there is no breeze,
It's that hot I don't think I'll freeze,
The rock stands in the sea nearby,
The sun passes along up above high,
I think I'll get my snorkle and face-mask,
In some sort of way I'll go on a task . . .

and so it continues for another twenty lines, all ending with a comma. There are various approaches for a teacher to take. One is to ask the pupil to try this poem without rhyme; another is to pursue the rhyming element by breaking the poem into stanzas (try couplets, quatrains, sestets etc.). Another approach is to focus on the uniformity of the line pattern and to re-consider the punctuation in its relation to the lines. Yet another is to accept the MacGonagall-like insistence and to aim to enhance the humorous aspects of the rhyme and rhythm.

There are other approaches, and the particular one chosen will depend on the child. One important point to bear in mind is that the poem is the child's, not the teacher's, and should not be appropriated. Negotiations with the writer, while always aiming to operate in the 'zone of proximal development' (Vygotsky 1986) should nevertheless remain true to the Gravesian principle of the 'ownership' of the text. That principle is not always followed.

David Holbrook (1981), for example, quotes the draft of a ten-year-old poet whose work had been generated in one of his workshops:

It has just begun to,
turn dark,
from the hill you can see,
All the lights being
turned on.
And the church bells,
ring for evening service.

and then comments (p. 35):

> I can't think why she wants to put commas like that at the end of lines. We can sort that out later; when I read the poem out it is clear enough, and its achievement becomes evident.

It is clear from Holbrook's printing of the poem how *he* thinks the poem should be read:

> It has just begun to turn dark.
> From the hill you can see
> All the lights being turned on
> And the church bells ring for evening service.

But if we look again at the child's initial draft, we can perhaps speculate as to whether she did in fact intend the line arrangement. The commas, I would suggest, are there to indicate and reinforce line endings even though they are grammatically incorrect. On three occasions, a verb comes at the beginning of a poetic line. These verbs happen to be the pivotal words in the three sentences that constitute the poem. Perhaps this is how she intended the poem to read:

> It has just begun to
> turn dark.
> From the hill you can see
> all the lights being
> turned on.
> And the church bells
> ring for evening service.

The only way to find out what she intended would have been to ask her to read the poem aloud rather than appropriate the experience.

In 'Shaping a poem', David Young (1975) describes several ways in which his Year 7 pupils moved towards final drafts, from notated poetic fragments:

> The grass is shiny green
> Lots of dead leaves
> Reed around edge of water
> Ripples = crossed

and prose catalogues:

> Red golds all leave look soggy. Raft in pond, fish in pond, reeds in pond, soggy apple. Clear inlet for water. Bike pedal in water. Acorn trees in water looks deep outlet. Falling leaves. Toadstools. ˙

It is impossible to generalize as to a single approach to drafting and editing in the writing of poetry. Each text and each writer is different; what is driving the shape of the text is the urgency of what is being said, or of what is trying to be said. Too slavish an attitude towards drafting can spoil work that in its first appearance on the page is better than in its polished or bungled later versions. We would do well to bear in mind James Britton's conviction in 'Shaping at the point of utterance' (1982: p. 140) that:

> successful writers adapt ... inventiveness and continue to rely on it rather than switching to some different mode of operating. Once a writer's words appear on the page, I believe they act primarily as a stimulus to *continuing* – to further writing, that is – and not primarily as a stimulus to *re-writing*.

On the other hand, there is no point in ruling out drafting as a possible strategy in the composing of poems. Alberta Turner's (1982: p. 55) statement that

> I'll discourage assigning first drafts of poems for homework. The poem, unlike the essay, doesn't benefit from being planned

seems not to recognize that the drafts of poems do not usually take the form of plans, but of beginnings, searchings after a rhythmic pattern, explorations, refinings, extensions, false trails and editings. Often, 'the point of utterance' can be extended over a longish period of composition, with varying degrees and kinds of concentration.

Other aspects of the relationship between speech and poetry

As already suggested, it is not part of the intention of this book to focus on developing responses to poetry, to ways of reading it and/or of 'bringing it off the page'. These are all crucially important factors in the life of poetry in schools, and they are dealt with in Stibbs and Newbould (1983), Dias and Hayhoe (1988), Benton *et al.* (1988), Protherough (1984) and in other books and articles However, it must be pointed out that if the impulse to poetry and the drive to poetic form begins in speech, so too does it benefit from being returned to speech in the form of readings, performances, dramatizations and discussions. The performance of poetry is something to bear in mind in its composition; more than ever, the poetic text will be like a script.

A pure form of poetry that is both aural and oral is sound poetry, and degrees of poetry between sound poetry and the more usual type of poetry (in which the meaning is more in focus than the sound of the words). Jonathon Williams's 'A Chorale of Cherokee Night Music' (reprinted in *Creatures Moving*, Summerfield 1970) acts as both a script for performance and a model for composition. Here is its beginning, though it continues for fourteen such lines:

> wahuhu wahuhu wahuhu wahuhu whauhu wahuhu wahuhu
> uguku uguku uguku uguku uguku uguku uguku uguku uguku
> huhu huhu huhu huhu huhu huhu huhu huhu huhu huhu huhu

This kind of writing can act as the spur to the composition of similar poems depicting the sounds of cities, towns or local neighbourhoods. Sound poems of a more specific and less potentially choral kind, like these by pupils in schools, can also be created:

Engine starting

Chuck a chuck chuck chuck chuch
Boom bang a chuck chuck BANG!
Chuckkkkk bang chuck chuck
brammmmmmmmamam a chuck a chuck chuck chuck
Brummmmmm (fast) chuckchuckchuckchuckchuckchuck
chuckchuckchuck hummmmmmmmmmmmme

(Matthew Dalton)

Splatter chutter chutter
chugger plugger
cough grunt
clugger clugger
ninger blicko
drucks stucka
stall FRUCKARISH
nukarish boweig
　crig

(Stephen Taylor)

and one can draw on the work of poets like Edwin Morgan, with his 'Loch Ness Monster's Song' or 'Canedolia', based on Scottish place names which are transposed into different parts of speech. In answer to the question 'what do you do?':

we foindle and fungle, we bonkle and meigle and maxpoffle. we
scotstarvit, armit, wormit, and even whifflet.

or on nonsense verse like 'Jabberwocky'.

Nonsense and absurd poetry are a vast source of pleasure and possibility for pupils in schools, building on rhymes and chants from early childhood. Margaret Meek has pointed out how comic and nonsense verse enable children to test the borders between sense and nonsense in language and in life. There is a real case here for seeing language as almost a world unto itself, though of course nonsense is always defined – however tenuously – in relation to sense of some kind. Freedom from conventionally recognized meaning is a territory that poetry is well-equipped to explore, as Robert Lowell indicated in his 'Afterthought' to *Notebook* (1970: p. 262):

I lean heavily to the rational, but am devoted to unrealism. An unrealist must not say, 'The man entered a house,' but, 'The man entered a police-whistle,' or 'Seasick with marital happiness, the wife plunges her eyes in her husband swimming like vagueness on the grass.'. . . Unrealism can degenerate into meaninglessness, clinical hallucinations or rhetorical machinery, but the true unreal is about something, and eats from the abundance of reality.

And nonsense and unrealism stumble effortlessly into metaphor, of which more in Chapter 8. One traditional poem that works well in this way is 'I'll have the whetstone', reprinted in *Voices* (Summerfield 1968) and elsewhere, a poem whose origin is in competitions to tell the tallest story:

> Hey, hey, hey, hey!
> I'll have the whetstone if I may.
>
> I saw a dog soaking sowse,
> And an ape thatching a house,
> And a pudding eating a mouse.
>   I'll have the whetstone if I may . . .

Work based on this poem with a Year 7 class is described in 'Poetry and the impossible' (Andrews 1978).

Playground rhymes, dialect poems, raps, lyrics, praises and curses, charms and spells – and even speeches – all come within this rich fund of oral forms (or 'speech genres') that contribute to and can inform poetry.

7 The visual dimension

If I paint what I know, I bore myself. If I paint what you know, I bore you. So I paint what I do not know.

Franz Klein

I intend in this chapter to interpret 'visual' broadly, to include the look of a poem on a page as well as the more localized meaning of 'visual' poetry, i.e. 'concrete poetry', 'shape poems' and so on. This breadth is an important principle to establish, because all too often the visual dimension to poetry is taken for granted. This complacency means that we not only do not 'see' the visual qualities of poems, but also that we are not open to the possibilities that such an insight offers us in the composition of poems in schools. What follows, then, is an exposition of ways into poetry that embraces the conventional approaches of observing and using the senses, but also includes the popular acrostics and alphabet poem forms as well as less commonly used techniques like slow motion and backwards poems (based on filmic principles), found poetry and concrete poetry (including collage and 'multi-panelled works') – more fully than is usually the case in the employment of 'shape poems'.

Let us then reconsider the visual dimension of poetry. Desite the predominantly oral and aural nature of the poem as a 'speech act', there is an inherently visual quality to this genre. If conscious rhythmic shaping is one of the defining features of the poem, then its representation on the printed page – its translation into the visual mode – is the reflection of that. It might even be possible to say that the rhythmic shape of the poem in the air can be determined by how the poem takes shape on the page, in the act of composition. Conversely, artists like Saul Steinberg have depicted speech in inventive and amusing ways: as music, as a ragbag of punctuation marks, as discordant configurations.

We have already mentioned that a poem is instantly recognizable from some distance simply on account of its layout. This layout acts as a score, just as a musical score acts as the basis of performance. But the visual shape of the poem on the page is worthy of exploration and study too, even though it is a secondary feature of poetry, a second order level of representation. It can have a life of its own, generate its own tensions and excitements, and give rise to its own range of possibilities.

Concrete poetry

'Concrete' poetry – poetry that focuses more on the visual aspect of the medium of communication than other poetry – is now a well-established tradition, as represented by anthologies like Bann (1967) or Williams (1967).

Like other kinds of poetic form, it flourishes outside Britain rather more happily than inside, locked as we are into a particular view of what constitutes poetry. It was avant-garde, but now has taken its place as another form of poetic communication.

What is striking about the anthologies of concrete poetry is their range. We tend in British schools to go as far as the visual representation of a single word, like

not pursuing this line into poems that take the principle much further, like Seiichi Niikuni's 'river/sandbank' (Fig. 2). This poem is quoted in an essay by Edwin

Figure 2   Seiichi Niikuni: 'kawa/sasu' kawa = river sasu = sand-bank

Morgan (1974), 'Into the Constellation', in which he traces the origin of concrete poetry 'as a conscious movement in the art of language' to 1955, in the work of the Noigandres group of poets in Sao Paulo and that of Gomringer and his circle in Ulm, though there are plenty of antecedents to the movement. It can be seen, in general terms (via its formalist tendencies), to be anti-expressionist and even to be part of the search for a new metric pattern, but as Morgan points out, expressiveness and rhythmic identity can also play their part in it. Given that this movement raised awareness about the typography of the page, liberating the text from the confines of the printer's demands and refocusing our attention on the whole work, perhaps the wordprocessor will enable students in school to experiment and play with the shapes that words make. Certainly, the potential is there, as indicated in this statement by Mallarmé (1897), quoted at the end of Morgan's article:

> The genre which [spatial poetry] may become, little by little, like the symphony compared to the monody, leaves intact the old style of verse, toward which I retain the greatest respect and attribute the sovereignity of passion and of dreams; while this [i.e. spatial poetry] would be the preferred manner for dealing (just as it follows) with subjects of the pure and complex imagination or intellect: which there is no reason any longer to exclude from Poetry . . .

Concrete poems can range on a scale from the purely typographic, through a type where poetic form itself is supplied by the visual arrangement of 'meaningful' words on the page, as in Herbert's 'Easter Wings':

> Lord, who createdst man in wealth and store,
>   Though foolishly he lost the same,
>   Decaying more and more,
>   Till he became
>   Most poore:
>   With thee
>   O let me rise
>   As larks, harmoniously,
>   And sing this day thy victories:
> Then shall the fall further the flight in me.
>
> My tender age in sorrow did beginne:
>   And still with sickness and shame
>   Thou didst so punish sinne,
>   That I became
>   Most thinne.
>   With thee
>   Let me combine,
>   And feel this day thy victorie:
> For, if I imp my wing on thine,
> Affliction shall advance the flight in me.

They can also take the form of collages (close in origin to 'found poems', discussed later), either in their raw form with words and phrases cut from various sources simply stuck on to the page in a particular sequence, or taken a stage further and made to appear like conventionally typeset poems, as in Adrian Mitchell's 'Vroomph! or The Popular Elastic Waist' and 'What the Mermaid Told Me' (1982).

Articles worth referring to on concrete poetry and in general on the relation between word and image are Stanley Cook's 'Seeing Your Meaning' (1978) and Michael Shaw's 'Word and Image – Mixed Ability Poetry?' (1982). Both stress the delights of representing meaning in readily accessible visual form, and of displaying such poems on the walls of the school.

'Computer' poetry

By 'computer poetry', I mean not poems composed on a word processor, but a poetry generated by a computer from a number of grammatical categories. 'Computer', then, is used as a metaphor for mechanistic sequences generated from a set of words. This is effected by drawing up a grid based on a grammatical sequence in English, for example:

The	crazy	moon	stalks	through	a	filthy	sky

Once the grid is in place, children can fill in each column with as many words as they can think of that fit there. It is clear, without having to spell it out, that the first column is headed by a definite article but could include other parts of speech that would also seem right in that place in the sentence, like 'many' or 'several' or 'a' or 'six'. The second column will consist of adjectives, the third of nouns, and so on. Once the grids are full of words, the 'computer' can then select random sequences and array them on the page next to each other, like so:

The crazy moon stalks through a filthy sky
Five black mornings wake in a heavy daze.
One beautiful face looms behind the magnificent wardrobe . . .

This approach gives rise to surreal combinations of words; it is meanings generated by words rather than the other way round, and suffers from the criticism made of Eliot by Pound in the drafts of 'The Waste Land': 'Il cherchait des sentiments pour les accommoder à son vocabulaire' (Eliot 1971: p. 11); but, on the other hand, it is an amusing and enjoyable way to generate some lines that can be argued over (for their grammatical and semantic qualities) and rearranged to see what meanings can be discovered in the various sequences.

Edwin Morgan, whose work we will refer to several times in this chapter, has written 'computer poems' that explore these possibilities, for example 'The Computer's First Christmas Card', 'The Computer's Dialect Poems' and other 'programmed' works (see Morgan 1982). And less metaphorically, there is now computer software on the market which deliberately exploits such flexibility in language.

Still and moving images

Poetry this century has borrowed much from photography (still images) and film (moving images), and the particular contribution of the Imagist movement will be reviewed later in this chapter. In contemporary terms, the poetry of Edwin Morgan has drawn heavily on photography – not in any parasitical sense, but in exploring common ground between the two art forms, and in particular similarities in ways of looking. One similarity, for example, is based on the notion that like a photograph, a poem often attempts to capture a single moment of experience – or to use Pound's phrase about an image in a poem, describing it as 'that which presents an intellectual and emotional complex in an instant of time' (Pound 1951a: p. 288). Voznesensky's 'Nostalgia for the Present' (in the volume of the same name, 1980) focuses on this same problem, using a number of images. Perhaps Morgan's *Instamatic Poems* (1972) illustrate this principle most clearly and accessibility. This small collection, some of which is included in the more readily available *Poems of Thirty Years* (1982), consists of a series of dated poems, each of which captures a particular moment. These moments are described or presented in the present tense (the implied, but not the actual tense of most lyric poetry) and read like accounts of photographs. Some of them extend to thirty or so lines. Here are some openings:

> It is opening night at Paolozzi's
> crashed car exhibition . . .
> > ('London June 1970')

> Nine hundred and sixty-eight pigs
> are running amok through a farm . . .
> > ('Seend Wiltshire April 1972')

> With a ragged diamond
> of shattered plate-glass
> a young man and his girl
> are falling backwards into a shop-window . . .
> > ('Glasgow 5 March 1971')

Students could either work from actual photographs or from memory to create these poems. Just as creating a past and future to a photograph gives a narrative dimension to the moment, so concentrating on the moment itself allows a poetic perspective to develop.

Another principle that can be linked to that of the photograph is that of observation. It is a principle embodied in the opening of Isherwood's *Goodbye to Berlin* (1939: p. 13):

> From my window, the deep solemn massive street. Cellar-shops where lamps burn all day, under the shadow of top-heavy balconied facades, dirty plaster frontages embossed with scroll-work and heraldic devices. The whole district is like this: street leading into street of houses like shabby monumental safes crammed with the tarnished valuables and second-hand furniture of a bankrupt middle-class.
>
> I am a camera with its shutter open, quite passive, recording, not thinking . . .

and in Douglas Dunn's allusively titled 'I am a Cameraman' (1974):

> They suffer, and I catch only the surface.
> The rest is inexpressible, beyond
> What can be recorded. You can't be them . . .

This principle of cool, dispassionate observation is – we all know – relative, but it remains a useful device for sharpening the observational (largely visual) sense, but also as an exemplary mode for the other senses to record or create what is there. As we have already noted in Chapter 3, the emphasis on honing the senses and the imagination was one of the driving forces of the creative writing movement. The important pedagogical feature of the approach described here is that the camera metaphor gives the writer a ready-made 'frame' through which to observe; this frame – or more precisely, aperture – is adjustable and allows variation in the degree of light one admits on to a subject, just as 'focus' enables the writer to bring the subject into close detail or to aim for a general impression. As in the best writing to emerge from the creative writing movement approach or from the researches of the London Writing Project, there is no shortage of expressiveness or disciplined observation: the two are not mutually exclusive. In a sense, we are finding ourselves returning to the position of Ruskin, as quoted on p. 19.

Another way in which word and image can be combined is by using photographs to stimulate the writing of poems. One such approach has been employed by students and teachers at the South Australian College of Advanced Education, who suggest the following activity:

1 Groups of 4–5 students receive a black and white photograph, showing people in a particular time/place.
2 Each student looks carefully at the picture allocated to the group, and lets thought 'free-float', jotting down ideas/impressions as they arise (5 minutes).
3 Each student then uses the collected responses, grouping, selecting, elaborating and structuring them into a poem which comments on the picture (15 minutes).
4 Still in the small group, students read poems to each other, select the poem they consider the most successful, and establish why.
5 Each group elects a reader to present poem, picture and critical justification to the full group. Discussion centres on the ways in which 'success' was judged.

Photographs can also be used to promote in-rôle writing, as described in the previous chapter, or combined in sequences to suggest stories, as in Berger and Mohr's *Another Way of Telling* (1980).

Before going on to discuss poetry's relationship to the moving image, let us first dwell for a moment on the Imagist contribution to the field. It will be important, not just for its contribution to the power of the 'image', but also for the part it played in the formulation of a new poetic in twentieth century British and American poetry. The name 'Imagiste' was coined in 1912 by Pound to describe the embryonic 'movement' that was gathering around the work of F. S. Flint, T. E. Hulme and others. The pre- and early history of the movement is well summarised in Press (1969), but the important features of the poems that come within this movement, as far as we are concerned, are their brevity and 'unevaluated' directness in the presentation of images, their 'hard, light, clear edges' (Pound 1951a: p. 78), their tendency to resemble 'sculpture rather than music' (Hulme 1955: p. 75). Despite this emphasis on the visual – a poetry resembling sculpture, photography or painting – the poems approximated music in their form, most of them appearing in free verse (though the association was not essential), and indeed Pound's 'to compose in the sequence of the musical phrase, not in sequence of a metronome' (1951: p. 288) was one of the principles of the movement. The other two were 'direct treatment of the "thing", whether subjective or objective' and 'To use absolutely no word that does not contribute to the presentation' (ibid.).

If Imagism as a movement fell apart in the late 1910s, it still had plenty to offer in practice in the shape of poems written under its broad umbrella and in these principles which enabled writers to cut through neo-Georgian verbiage and – by implication – swathes of post-Swinburnian 'feeling' and sentimentality. If we read 'image' for 'thing' in the following passage from Wei T'ai, we will get a clear summary of the advice that might have come from the Imagist movement at its best:

> Poetry presents the thing in order to convey the feeling. It should be precise about the thing and reticent about the feeling, for as soon as the mind regrounds and connects with the thing, the feeling shows in the words: this is how poetry enters deeply within us.

Here is an early Imagist poem, T. E. Hulme's 'Above the Dock':

> Above the quiet dock in midnight,
> Tangled in the tall mast's corded height,
> Hangs the moon. What seemed so far away
> Is but a child's balloon, forgotten after play.

It will be seen that this kind of poetry, with its brevity, spare imagery, economy of expression and focusing on the 'thing' rather than the feeling (i.e. subject rather than writer), has a good deal in common with haiku, waka and other oriental verse forms. These have been consistently popular in schools in the last twenty-five years or so, not least for the fact that their brevity makes them accessible to a wide range of writers within each class. Haiku, for example, can be written in either a loose 'three-line' version, or in the more strict syllabic structure of five-seven-five, as in the following example:

> The climber's pack squats
> like a gravestone in the snow:
> his prints fill slowly.

These tight forms are useful for the editing that they induce in the writer's mind as he or she tries to find the most appropriate words to fit the meaning and syllabic structure. But more than this, the poems demonstrate a compression of observation and feeling in a complete, if minute, form. As explained in the last chapter with regard to renga, these poems can be written alongside waka and other Chinese and Japanese forms and combined into chains to form longer poems.

Pound championed the cause of the image further in his edited notes of Fenollosa (1936), *The Chinese Written Character as a Medium for Poetry*. These have been ridiculed by sinologists and other scholars, but their contribution to an awareness of the *poetic* potential of the Chinese character remains unquestioned. Essentially, they aim to demonstrate that the Chinese character, because of its assumed origins as a pictographic medium, retains a close affinity with the source object, however abstract its reference. So, for example, the chief verb for 'is' not only means 'to have' (p. 15):

> but shows by its derivation that it expresses something even more concrete, namely 'to snatch from the moon with the hand'. Here the baldest symbol of prosaic analysis is transformed by magic into a splendid flash of concrete poetry.

When we move on to moving images, further poetic possibilities suggest themselves. The fact that films are composed of single images following each other, frame by frame, can be applied to the writing of poetry. If we take a number of 'frames' from a filmic sequence – in effect a series of stills – the analogy we can make with poetry is with a series of stanzas working towards the expression of a single theme. The resulting poem gets its energy from the juxtaposition of 'images', as it were, rather as in Eliot's 'Preludes', and can take narrative or collage-like form.

This principle of juxtaposition, while not fully analogous to the running of film, does have connections with the composition of image with image and one of the crucial creative acts in the making of a film: editing. It is as though one is able to write short fragments and then put them together to say something more substantial. This is why weaker writers can gain success in the composition of poetry: there is no requirement to sustain writing for a long period or across a whole page. Poetic fragments can act as the building blocks to larger structures. Classics of juxtaposition, apart from 'The Waste Land', *The Cantos*, 'Briggflatts' and other poems out of most students' reach as writers, are Wallace Stevens' 'Thirteen Ways of Looking at a Blackbird' (Stevens 1953) and, in a different

way, Miroslav Holub's sequences of short poems, like 'Brief reflections on . . .'
(1984).

Workshops can be built around this approach. For example, something can be
used as the focus of attention for a group of students (e.g. a bird in a cage, a brick,
a vase of flowers, a machine). Each of the students writes notes about the subject
in poetic shorthand for, say, ten minutes; then they compare notes, polish their
own fragments and attempt to compose them into a whole. This can also be
attempted with each writer composing the whole poem by him or herself (and
choosing his or her own subject), or indeed in parodies of the Stevens poem
('Thirteen Ways of Looking at Homework', 'Thirteen Ways of Not Looking at
Your Parents'). It is probably best to try this approach collaboratively at first, and
then to move on to individual compositions.

Another way of coming close to the elusive present is via an analogy with
slow-motion film. A single line is written, describing a moment of action like a car
crash, a reunion or someone waiting at a streetcorner for his date:

> I stand at the corner, waiting for her.

This line is then doubled, to make a composition of two lines:

> I stand at the corner of the street, waiting
> for the girl who probably won't come.

These lines, in turn, are doubled to make four. Each time the doubling takes
place, the effort should try to be to retain focus on the one situation or incident
that is at the heart of the poem; it is possible to retain existing lines and simply add
more information about the scene, or to describe the actions (or inactions) in
more detail:

> I stand at the corner of the street, waiting
> for the girl who probably won't come.
> She is already late, the evening's disappearing
> and I stare at the cracks in the pavement.

Obviously, each time the lines are doubled, the writing gets more difficult. Some
young writers will be able to get as far as eight lines:

> I stand at the corner of High Street
> outside the Cannon cinema,
> waiting for the girl who won't come.
> She is late, the evening's half gone,
> and I begin to pretend we hadn't agreed
> to meet for a film and a bite to eat.
> I stare at the cracks in the pavement,
> my mind wandering, my heart near my feet.

What is interesting about this approach is that if the concentration is maintained
on the single scene, situation or moment, the expansion that takes place in the
poem brings about an exploration of the feelings involved. There is also a great

deal of shaping and re-shaping that goes on; for instance although, up to now, the lines have been slightly adapted each time, it is possible as we move to sixteen lines to leave the first eight intact.

As the poem gets longer, different compositional questions arise. How much new information is going to be included? Is a narrative going to emerge? Should there be some structuring of the composition into stanzas? It is possible to extend this approach to thirty-two, sixty-four lines and beyond; and of course one does not have to double the length of the poem each time; this is merely a device for generating an intriguing text.

Another filmic approach which works well in prose or verse is to envisage film running backwards. This has the effect of breaking down assumptions about narrative sequence, making you rethink the causal and temporal relationship between separate actions. The idea was first suggested to me by a passage from Kurt Vonnegut's *Slaughterhouse Five* (1970) in which Billy Pilgrim imagines the American bombing of a German city *backwards*:

> American planes, full of holes and wounded men and corpses took off backwards from an airfield in England. Over France, a few German fighter planes flew at them backwards, sucked bullets and shell fragments from some of the planes and crewmen. They did the same for wrecked American bombers on the ground, and those planes flew up backwards to join the formation . . .

There is also an Ian Seraillier poem that tells a fairy story backwards, and a poem by Gunter Künert, 'Film Put in Backwards' (in Hamburger 1972 and Andrews 1983) based on the same principle. Not only does writing in this way make one reconsider the temporal and causal relationships between events, but the moral tenor of those conventional narrative sequences is altered. We realise that most stories are moving quite firmly along moral and emotional lines. Added to these potential revelations is the sheer fun of conceiving something happening in reverse:

> Piece by piece
> the builders are taking down our house:
> first they start on the inside,
> carefully taking the wallpaper off in strips.
> Then the lightbulbs, which are
> put back in boxes and returned to the local shop.
> Our furniture, books and toys
> are taken to a big van and driven off
> backwards out of sight.
> The plaster comes off with a trowel,
> the wires are stripped out,
> pipes and lagging removed.
> Then the roof slates fly back
> into the hands of builders' lads,
> the walls come down, brick by brick
> and all is made flat again.

Triptych

She is standing on a balcony
somewhere in Italy. On the parapet
is a vase of dried flowers,

when suddenly comes an angel.
This one's got wings
and a golden ice-skating blade
for skimming through space;
ribbons blazing, with one hand
braking, the other raised to greet.

No wonder she looks scared.
Hands held up in defence,
but the angel dives in.

What would it be like,
to be crashed into by an angel?
Your stomach would jump –
it would be like falling in love.
Your clothes would fall away.
Suddenly you feel your fingers
wrapped in light. Your body
unravels,

your metabolism moving so fast,
atoms explode in the microwave,
you disappear from sight.
It's all happening at the speed of light.

This seems impossible
but there he goes –
all 240lb of St Paul
already about six feet up
and on his way to Hotel Paradis.

They've left his sword & books,
his passport, his wallet, his Access card
abandoned, as in a fire alarm.

Three hefty C17 angels,
wings just starting to beat
(each about 190lb)
move him upwards as if he were
a model in polystyrene.

It is an angel hovering
ten feet above the prison door.
Someone has dropped to his knees.
Another turns to stare at a blank wall.
The bottom half of this vision
– which nobody sees –
is a rocket launcher burning;
the top half, a man.

He seems to have blasted
a hole in the prison wall.
The prisoners are running for it.
And he hovers like a Chinook in a gale,
like a hummingbird on the edge of heaven.

And I say, ten feet above ground level,
while a shattering of stone,
a freeing from fetters,
shutters, curtains, blinds
are dropping from eyes
and everyone runs shouting into the street.

(Ranieri (1423–1450), 'La Liberation
des prisonnieres de Florence par
le Bienheureux')

And when you come to,
and find your feet again,
the cool marble floor speaks to you,
the vase is filled with fresh flowers
and teeters on the edge of the balcony.
Catch it, quick!

Look up and see nothing.
A few trails of vapour, a summer.

And here you are again,
on the street, and you can speak again,
and the vase is teetering on the edge of the balcony
but for the moment
you have nothing –
absolutely nothing –
to say.

(Braccesso (1478–1501), 'L'Annonciation')

The look on his face is a mixture of
'Hey, what is this?' and
'Come on you guys, be serious'
with just a touch of
'I had a feeling this would happen'
and 'In two seconds I'll be enjoying this'.

Of course, he won't fully let go
until he's well and truly
checked in upstairs –
holiday of a lifetime (more)
all expenses paid.

(Poussin (1594–1665),
'Le Ravissement de St Paul')

Figure 3

Yet another way of extending the principle of different viewpoints is to explore the notion of what the French call 'polyptiques' or multi-panelled works, applying it to poetic composition. The most common form of polyptique is the triptych, a work of three panels. Seamus Heaney, for instance, has not only composed several poems in sections, but has one called 'Triptych'.

The principle can be applied to poetry in the following way. Composition on a particular theme or subject can take the form of separate statements or 'bursts' of writing. Whereas in conventional poetic composition, the pressure is always to reach some kind of unity – to make everything cohere – the separate sections that are created in this approach can retain their integrity. When it is felt that there is nothing more to say, the various sections (from two upwards) can be arrayed, and then arranged to form a satisfying whole. This arrangement can be linear or spatial (see Fig. 3). As Edgar Allan Poe has suggested, what we term a long poem is often merely a succession of brief ones.

The poetry of Edwin Morgan

Edwin Morgan's work warrants a section to itself because, probably more than any other modern British writer, his inventiveness seems to offer a good deal to students, particularly those who are in danger of being disaffected with poetry. Morgan is one of the poets who is able to break through this lack of interest and speak to adolescents with a fresh and challenging voice.

I suspect the reasons for the disaffection are manifold. One will be a move away from delight in regular rhythms and rhyming, which will be associated with the innocent pleasures of childhood. Another will be a dissatisfaction with the common subjects and themes of poetry, particularly with poems that attempt to convey feeling or which dwell on emotions. Yet another will be the growing out of delight in the zanier, humorous verse of Milligan and others in favour of a sharper, more socially- and politically-based, more satirical humour. Morgan's work, though it stands very much in the tradition of British writing, has other qualities which appeal to those disaffected with poetry.

One of these qualities is the nature of subject matter. It is the fact that several of Morgan's poems are about space and science fiction. Arguably his best collection is *From Glasgow to Saturn* (1973) which, along with a range of other poems, includes 'Interferences', 'The First Men on Mercury' and 'Spacepoem 3 – Off Course'. Then there is *Star Gate* (1979), a volume subtitled 'Science Fiction Poems', including an 'instamatic' about the moon, particle and clone poems, a list poem ('Foundation') which asks 'What would you put in the foundation-stone/ for future generations?' and a striking sequence of five poems called 'The Moons of Jupiter' which are written in the first-person, in rôle, as a traveller:

> Boots and boats – in our bright orange gear
> we were such an old-fashioned earthly lot
> it seemed almost out of time-phase.

Few poets write about space or in science fiction mode: it has been assumed perhaps that the genre is the province of prose.

But it is not even the subject matter of Edwin Morgan's poems that offers most to the secondary (and primary!) school student; it is rather the experimentation with form. Many of the space poems take unusual form, for example the well-anthologized 'First Men on Mercury' which uses the question-and-answer format, or the less well-known 'countdown' poem in the 'Interferences' sequence. Perhaps most arresting in form are the 'Emergent Poems', included in the collected edition and appearing in other collections. Other poems worth looking up for possible use in class are 'The Suspect' (1968) with its dislocated lines reflecting the state of mind and the voice of the suspect:

Asked me for a match suddenly/with his hand up
I thought he was after my wallet
gave him a shove/he fell down

sound, shape and computer poems already mentioned, and 'Sir Henry Morgan's Song' (1977) which takes the form of a series of simple metamorphoses:

we came to the boat and blew the horn
we blew the boom and came to the island
we came to the innocent and cut the cackle . . .

A recent collection, *Themes on a Variation* (1988), includes a section of 'news-poems', 'cut out from newspapers and other ephemeral material, pasted on to sheets of paper, and photographed' (p. 62). These are either 'found' intact and lifted from their original context to take on new significance in a poetic arena, or rearranged, cut or adapted in some way to deliver a message. Morgan calls them 'inventions', 'both in the old sense of "things found" and in the more usual sense of "things devised"'. An example appears on p. 16.

Found poetry

Found poetry is almost always primarily visual. 'Heard' poetry – as in Doolittle's 'native woodnotes wild' in *Pygmalion* – exists and can be captured in print or act as the seed or catalyst to a poetic composition. What is usually 'found' is not a pre-existing poem, but a text or part of a text that does not know it is poetic. Thus, in visual terms, inscriptions on gravestones, the texts of advertisements (particularly the long texts of advertisements in colour supplements, newspapers and magazines), letters where poetic shape is latent, and newspaper articles are some of the texts where poetry might be found. Finding it is a matter of keeping an eye trained (and half an ear tuned) to poetic possibility; lifting it from its context and setting it within parameters – both visual and contextual – is what makes it into poetry.

One of the best essays on found poetry is by Nancy Gorrell (1979). In it, she describes a series of lessons with her class based on Julius Lester's poem 'Parents', published in *Search for a New Land: History of Subjective Experience*

(1969). In the first lesson, she lets the students read the poem by themselves, and then after a discussion, shows them the article from the *New York Times* on which the poem is based. After further discussion, they are sent off to 'find' their own poems from any non-literary source. These are copied and circulated around the class in the next lesson, and are used as the basis for a discussion about the nature of poetry. While I cannot agree that Gorrell's checklist to test the poeticality of the Lester poem is particular to poetry, suffering as it does from the same focus on *effect* that some of the definitions we consider in Chapter 2 suffer from (e.g. 'is the poem evocative and empathetic?', 'Is the language excited?' etc.), it remains an important discovery (p. 34) that found poetry:

> lets students connect to what excites, outrages, inspires, and provokes them in the real world. It starts where they are, and lets them respond with passion. It provides a vehicle for attitudinal change – poetry is everywhere to be discovered. It makes students active observers and seekers developing their own poetic sensibilities. And last, it inspires students to write their own poems – the final and perhaps most important way of responding.

One might add that the attitudinal change, especially if the found texts are politically charged, might spread beyond a change in attitude towards poetry. The third lesson involves a further sharing of the found texts.

Lester selected from the original newspaper story rather than lifting it whole, and that is also the case with the following poem:

If Adam and Eve
walked east
of the Garden of Eden
today

they would cross
a
little
bridge

over
the river Jordan
and run
up

against the high steel security fence
and watchtowers
of the Kibbutz Bet Zera.

They would hit the road
and dodge between trailers
taking tanks to the Lebanese front.

They would hear the gentle rumble
of Israeli fighter-bombers
patrolling the Bekaa valley.

This is based on a report by David Blundy which appeared in *The Sunday Times* for 10th October, 1982, which begins with an epigraph from Genesis, and starts:

> If Adam and Eve walked east of the Garden of Eden today, as I did last week, they would find the view distinctly more prosaic . . .

This process of moving from found text to poem can be illustrated using several other sources. This extract from an advertisement for Renault cars not only is almost poetic in itself, but works on the same principle as a poem by Edwin Morgan, 'Off-Course':

> The power-assisted steering.
> The electro-magnetic door locking.
> The five-speed gearbox.
> The electric front windows.
> The hatchback.
> The tinted glass.
> The twin-choke Weber carburettor.
> The internal headlight adjuster
> The all-round independent suspension.

It is also redolent of, and a nice contrast to, a Raymond Carver poem, 'The Car' (1988), which starts:

> The car with a cracked windshield.
> The car that threw a rod.
> The car without brakes . . .

and which ends, after a litany of nearly fifty such statements:

> The car of my dreams.
> My car.

Another source is far from the world of advertising, but nevertheless is language at its most persuasive: speeches such as 'Chief Seattle's testimony', which contains statements like:

> Every part of this earth is sacred to my people.
> Every shining pine needle,
> every sandy shore,
> every mist in the dark woods,
> every clearing . . .

Whereas Julius Lester's poem relies on a narrative for its poetic structure, these texts (advertisements and speeches) rely on listing – one of the primitive poetic principles discussed earlier in the book. One extraordinary found poem is a 'Help the Aged' advertisement from the *Guardian* (Fig. 4). It not only tells a story but also employs the techniques of spacing words in order to convey the impact of its message.

When you're old you can become cold without even noticing it.
Often without so much as a shiver.

You simply slow down.

Soon you can't be bothered to make yourself
a proper meal. A slice of toast will do.
And why build up the fire? You feel all right.
You don't notice your body getting colder.

And you slow down.

The next thing you don't notice is your
mind slowing down. Did you order the
coal? You can't remember. Never mind.

Now you've really slowed down.

You feel drowsy. Even the effort

of going to bed seems too much.

You just nod off in the chair.

It doesn't seem to

matter any mor

Figure 4   Help the Aged advertisement

Alphabet poems, acrostics and other whims

Alphabet poems are a good way to start children writing poems, because the form
is simple and accessible, and builds on rhymes and mnemonics – and the sheer

rhythmic shape of some alphabet recitations – learnt from early childhood. The usual format is to see such poems based on alliterative sequences:

A is for albatross arching through air
B is for the brown, bad-tempered bear . . .

either ryhmed in couplets, as in this example, or unrhymed. Any subject can be used, though there tends to be a common theme to the list. But there is a much greater range of alphabet poems, as evidenced by Peter Mayer's collection *Alphabetical and Letter Poems* (1978). This includes poems like Alaric Watts' 'The Siege of Belgrade':

An Austrian army, awfully array'd,
Boldly by battery besiege Belgrade;
Cossack commanders cannonading come,
Deal devastation's dire destructive doom . . .

and the Shaker animal alphabet:

Alligator, beetle, porcupine, whale,
Bobolink, panther, dragonfly, snail,
Crocodile, monkey, buffalo, hare,
Dromedary, leopard, mud-turtle, bear . . .

both of which are examples of fairly regular metre enhanced by the relative lack of importance of sense. More than one line can be devoted to each letter, thus introducing variation into the poem, and as much as whole stanzas can work in this way, making for quite substantial texts. At the other end of the spectrum are Aragon's bleakly minimal 'Suicide' (simply a five-line printing out of the alphabet) and Holub's wittier 'Very Brief Thoughts on the Letter "m"' in which the 'm' is left out of the alphabet. It is also possible to give one letter to each of the members of a class to create variations on words beginning with that letter, or at least to start a poem with that letter; these can then be displayed, along with typographical and letter designs, around the room.

Also popular as ice-breakers and as ways to generate ideas at the beginning of each line are acrostics. These are often based on the names of the children writing them, but can branch out into portraits of other historical and topical figures, as well as other subjects, like:

S uddenly you find yourself on the streets
T rying to get support; you're like a beggar.
R ich people pass you by and ignore you:
I 'm alright, is their attitude. They'll happily
K ick you when you're down,
E ven tell the papers you've got no case . . .
S till, we're holding out. It's our pride that counts.

Acrostics are just one kind of typographical whim – a form popular in the nineteenth century, and with children.

The act of seeing

The visual dimension to poetry can include not only visual properties and organizing principles of texts, but also the act of seeing. By this, I do not mean merely the use of sight as one of the five senses, employed as data-collecting agents to supply the memory and imagination (a rather Augustan approach to poetics). The characterization of the *act* of seeing lifts the activity to a level which involves not passive reception of sense-data, but actual framing of vision. Perhaps because sight is our principal sense, we all too readily erect it as the metaphor for all imaginative activity without fully recognizing that imagination can involve all the senses. The very word, with 'image' at its root, is locked into this sight-bound way of seeing. In turn, the root of the word 'image' is associated with imitation.

There are various ways to induce an act of seeing without determining what is seen. None of these ways are the sole province of poetry, and as such must be seen as secondary features of the genre; they might just as easily appear in prose form. The reason for including them here is that they are such a part of the poetical viewpoint in our culture that to ignore them would be to limit the scope of the argument; not only that, but they are approaches which enlighten and excite in a particular way – one that has become associated with poetry itself. Metaphor and simile – those old stand-bys of poetic analysis – come into this category.

One approach that works to this effect is the notion of seeing something for the first time. This can be couched in the form of a visitor from another planet reporting back his or her perceptions of life on earth (cf. Craig Raine's *A Martian Sends a Postcard Home*, 1979), and is also a device used in films like *Crocodile Dundee* or *Being There*, where the respective heroes – one from the Australian outback and the other from incarceration in front of the television – enter a world (in both cases, New York) with the eyes of a *naif*. The key 'poetical' quality in all of these cases is that things that we take for granted, like the rules of a cricket match or the lighting and smoking of a cigarette, are seen – as it were – for the first time, and so have to be described in literal detail and at the same time compared to what the onlooker already knows. Analogy thus plays an important part in the process. The results are not dissimilar to the breaking down of simple actions into 'frames' as in the 'slow-motion' poems above, nor to riddles:

The Cricket Match

First everyone gets dressed up
in white clothes which they carry
in long, tube-like bags.
Those that are sacrificed
wear pads and bumpers over
all the points of their bodies,

then they walk to the middle
waving their weapons. Fierce ones
hurl missiles at them, which the
victims try to hit, to save their bacon;
but neither can escape, till tea is taken.

Where these recordings of an 'innocent' eye do come close to poetic form is in the halting rhythms of the perceptions, never quite sure what they are looking at and so never quite confident enough to fall into the more relaxed rhythms of prose.

Another device for seeing in a new and refreshing way is that of scale. When Lilliputians search Gulliver's pockets, they report their findings in a delightfully comical way:

In the right coat pocket of the great Man Mountain, after a thorough search, we found only one piece of coarse cloth, large enough to be a carpet for your Majesty's stateroom. In the left pocket, we saw a huge silver chest, with a silver cover, which we were not able to lift. We wanted to get into it; and one of us who stepped into it, found himself up to his knees in a sort of dust, some of which flew into our faces and got us all sneezing . . .

Again, the qualities of transformation and humour, as well as the riddle-like nature of the text, are evident. Scale is a greatly underestimated factor in the creation of figurative language, and a device used more often by poets than is sometimes acknowledged. Ted Hughes' 'A Cranefly in September' (1976) uses this device as the basis of a welter of images:

Her jointed bamboo fuselage,
Her lobster shoulders, and her face
Like a pinhead dragon, with its tender moustache,
And the simple colourless church windows of her wings

and it is also there in the observations of scientists like Robert Hooke on first looking through microscopes. Indeed, using microscopes to look closely at tiny objects is a way of beginning to explore metaphor.

Another act of imagination that provides a good deal of material to explore is making the visible invisible and vice-versa. Again, the dislocation brought about by rendering invisible particular objects can be both comic and revelatory:

I like to imagine
people in a plane
without the seats;
or on a train
zooming along
above the ground;
children on a roundabout
dancing round and round.
Everyone riding

on the air
looking quite happy
though there's nothing there

though the obverse of this approach, with the invisible being realized in the imagination, promises more, as in the beginning of this Eskimo poem (see p. 84):

There is a tribe of invisible men
who move around us like shadows – have you felt them?

These men are invisible while alive, but you can see their tracks and their weapons, and when they die they become visible.

These approaches are some of the ways in which metaphor and simile can be made accessible to children in primary and secondary schools. This brief survey does not pretend to be comprehensive in any way; what it is suggesting is that the visual dimension to poetry can offer ways into writing that, while not necessarily having to take poetic form, have much in common with certain ways in which poetry tends to operate. They are pre-poetic ways of seeing, devices which reveal some of the primal patterns and framings that underpin poetry.

It has also been part of the intention to put simile and metaphor in perspective[1]. We have been obsessed by these rhetorical devices in the consideration of poetry[2], almost asserting at times that they are the *sine qua non* of poetry. As has been made clear in Chapter 3, they formed the pillars of poetic practice in the creative writing movement, based on the assumptions that the development of the imagination and the expression of 'self' were the purposes of such writing. But it is clear that, as soon as we look outside the British tradition, we discover poems that employ neither similes nor metaphors, but speak with a direct voice: some of the poems of Carl Sandburg, Bertolt Brecht, Pablo Neruda and East Europeans like Miroslav Holub and Vasko Popa work in this way; of Voznesensky, Ratushinskaya and Akhmatova from Russia; many Japanese haiku or modern Chinese poems, and writing from South America and Africa can operate without metaphor.

One could argue that the very representation of experience, thoughts or feelings in words is itself metaphorical; that the words on the page, however direct they seem, 'stand for' something else. They are a 'second order symbolism' in their embodiment of the first order symbolism of speech. All of this is true, but it is stretching the definition of metaphor to call it metaphorical. Only in the broadest sense can we say that all language is metaphorical because of its symbolic nature.

If we follow this line of argument further, we could say that if language is symbolic, and if poetry is the 'highest', 'purest' form of language because of its self-referential nature, then poetry is the finest development of symbolic and metaphorical language available to us.

However, the second statement of this imperfect syllogism has already been proved to be one of the stumbling blocks of poetry, itself generated from the confusion between 'the effect and it', i.e. that the effects of poetry (inducing states of high feeling) are a result of the fact that poetry uses heightened language. We know now that poetry draws as much on the language of the world as any other form of discourse and that is it unhelpful to hive it off into some higher but remote realm. We also know that the 'heightened language' cannot be confined to metaphorical language, because this kind of language operates ubiquitously: stories, conversations, expletives, and political speeches can all draw on this metaphorical fund.

At the same time, the intention is not to minimize the power of metaphor. It remains – through its sheer fusing energy, its ability to shed new light on a subject, its perception of correspondence, its linking of big and small, its ability to cross over between the concrete and the abstract, its surprising and revelatory nature – one of the most exciting and life-giving features of the linguistic repertoire that poetry draws on.

Other approaches

Not all approaches to the writing and reading of poetry come under the oral/aural and visual dimensions, though these are convenient and very general ways of organizing such approaches. They were used because they are based on inherent qualities in poems, and are thus less subject to the vagaries of a 'reader-centred' or 'creative writing' approach; but they remain mere categories and not part of a pedagogical or theoretical model for the teaching of poetry.

There are still issues and practices to consider which do not fall easily into either of the categories, but which suggest further possibilities for developing poetry in the classroom. One of these is described by Thomas McKendy (1987), and consists of students writing consciously *bad* poetry to a Rod McKuen formula, and in this way alerting themselves to the specific features of such writing. Not only does this practice make for a good deal of humour when the poems are shared, but it raises the awareness of how formulaic poetry works and of the clichés that can fossilize feeling. A further exercise, once this initial encounter has made its points is to approximate 'good' writing – a kind of paraphrasing of particular passages – in order to gauge the reasoning behind the choice of words in the original. In both cases, there is a commitment on the part of the student writer alongside the work of the established writer, so that the apprentice feels he or she is part of a living craft where it matters that you use one word rather than another in a particular context.

This is one of the principal reasons for the practice of *writing* poetry in schools as well as reading. it. Few teachers ever work on the premise that they are trying to produce professional poets at eighteen or beyond. If they are, they have been singularly unsuccessful in achieving that aim. There is no systematic way of 'becoming a writer' and any number of lessons, workshops and manuals will not bring about the desired effect. The actual course to becoming an established writer is much less predictable than that, as the testimonies of writers in interviews prove: it seems more a matter of circumstance, desire, talent, hard work and chance. But creating professional poets and novelists is not the point of such programmes in school. Much more central is the aim to practise a craft in which every word counts, in which feelings and thoughts are given expression, and in which the creation of an art-object brings particular satisfactions. Added to these are the benefits that writing poetry brings to the reading of poetry, including the sense of practising a common craft, already mentioned above, and a *working knowledge* of the writerly/readerly text.

Another approach that enhances knowledge of texts is translation – or at least comparisons of different translations of the same text. This need not be as remote a possibility for use in a secondary school class as might first seem. As all students in the National Curriculum will be learning a second language up to the age of 16, the possibility of translation of European and other poems in English lessons is there. I suggest this happens in English lessons, because the benefits are likely to be greater for English than they are for the language being translated from; and the expertise of the English teacher in creating a unified and readable text will be needed. This will not be translation in the usual sense of rendering a passage as accurately and literally as is possible in another language, but translation in the wider sense of making a new text that will represent the original. A group of students working on the same text can compare their versions of the original and discuss the choices open to them.

If competence in another language is not sufficient to make a success of this approach, the technique described by Michael Kelly (1973) may prove useful. He gave his students two different translations of a Horace ode to consider. The first stanza of each was as follows:

I   What slender youth bedew'd with liquid odours
    Courts thee on Roses in some pleasant Cave,
       Pyrrha for whom bind'st thou
       In wreaths thy golden hair . . .

II What scented stripling, Pyrrha, wooes thee now
    In pleasant cavern, all with roses fair?
    For whom those yellow tresses bindest thou
       With simple care?

These are then compared to a third version:

III Pyrrha, what slender boy
         sprinkled with soft perfumes,
     within some pleasant cave
         courts you amid rose blooms?

and finally, after much discussion about the differences between the three versions, and on the nature of poetry and translation, a fourth version is thrown in for consideration, raising new issues about poetry and voice:

IV Baby, what guy is necking you right now in some alcove?
    Say, babe, who is that stiff? It's for him, kid, you doll
    up so neat . . . and say, that blonde hair!

Both this and the idea of writing bad verse are intertextual approaches to the study of poetry, as is parody. Developing the idea behind the last version of Horace's ode or the 'bad' verse can lead to parodies of particular poems. And as the art of parody is partly in treading a fine line between the original and the bathetic version, much will be learnt about the structure, wording and tone of the original poem.

There are two further approaches which almost always generate expressive writing, but which are probably best used with students of 13 and over. One is the 'memory chain', an approach developed by the New York City Writing Project. It usually leads to writing in prose, but can be channelled just as easily toward poetic form. In this method, students are asked first to note briefly a series of memories, each triggered by the previous one and the first triggered by some object, word or face in the room. In this stage of the process, the writing should be rapid – almost 'automatic' – with the minimum of editorial control or 'censorship' on the part of the writer. After a period of a few minutes, this process of association is stopped and students can discuss their chains in pairs, comparing the different acts and sequences of memory. Next, students are asked to focus on a particular part of their memory chain that seems to them to be important: something they might like to explore in writing. This might be a single topic, or it might be the central moment in a network of related topics that appear elsewhere in the chain.

Then follows a ten or fifteen minute period of rapid ('first draft') writing. If this approach is used to generate poems, a decision has to be made by the writer as to whether to seek poetic form from this point, or whether to write the initial draft in prose (as Yeats often did). As explored elsewhere in his book, the moment at which the decision is taken to move into poetic form is crucial, and the ultimate form of the poem may be determined by the rhythmic shape of a phrase or of a series of lines. Hereafter, the writing can continue with redraftings, discussions with other members of the writing group, reflections and so on, until the poem is completed.

Often this approach generates autobiographical work, as in these extracts from a poem by Harriet Bailer – an epic poem entitled 'The Bronx, my home' and composed in polyptical form:

1. Bryant Avenue

I wish I was born there,
not only raised there –
My grandma's house, my house.
I had a few toys, no friends, shared a bed,
had grandma's warm, sweet cooking,
and daily coffee.
Sugar cubes melting in my mouth.

When she called me 'Hatchculah', the birds would sing.

2. 179th Street

We made use of the hill between Bryant and Vyse.

Rollerskating down with Anise, Brucie and Anne,
going from rough concrete
to gray slippery slate
from safe wide surfaces
to scary, narrow ones,
planning or not
Our Stopping

at the very bottom.

3. The other side of the lake

That's where we would go
to throw our sins away.
On Yom Kippur,
we would dress up,
davin all day,
and by late afternoon,
gather all our misdeeds, shame and evil words
and cast them into the vigorous Bronx river.
We knew it was a river,
but every kid on our block
called this place
'the other side of the lake'.

4. 1975 Bathgate Avenue

Friday afternoons
piano lessons at Mrs Crimi's.
Waiting on her brocade couch
while Walter finished his hour.
Playing duets with him
while Mrs Crimi tapped her pencil in steady rhythm.
Then, my hour alone
with the black haired, fair skinned beauty.
I was in love with her voice,
the way she would turn a page,
write with sharpened pencils
delicate notes in my spiral book.
But nothing was wonderful
until Mrs Crimi began to play.
Chopin waltzes and nocturnes would fly from her hands,
her fingers like ballet dancers,
stretching and bending and soaring with grace.
My heart would beat faster,
my whispers would yell,
'Don't stop, don't stop.'

Another approach to writing in which the pressure to express can benefit from
playing with poetic form is writing from anger. Again, lists can act as the

starting-point, and trigger lines can be used if necessary ('Look at the way . . .', 'What I can't stand about . . .'). Here is an example of the beginning of such a poem, by Susan di Carlo:

Down with the generic 'he'

The royal HE does not reflect me
she/he; he/she/; s-slash-he
does not represent me.
From whence this he-man language comes?
I'd like to put it in a tomb.
SOON.

Notes

1 See David Trotter (1984) *The Making of the Reader.*
2 The best book on the rhetoric of poetry that I have come across, and in which simile and metaphor are considered alongside other devices at various linguistic levels, is *The Princeton Handbook of Poetic Terms* (Preminger *et al.* 1986).

8 The case for poetry

Poetry is a response to the daily necessity of getting the world right.

Wallace Stevens

Most of the justifications for the place of poetry in the school curriculum are overstated and oblique. It is hard to avoid such statements, however. Justifying all but the most narrowly functional or obviously beneficial disciplines is difficult, and because poetry seems to stand at the opposite end of the spectrum from the practical and useful, the task is made more difficult still. Furthermore, poetry is seen in some quarters as not just a verbal art, but as the jewel in the crown of the verbal arts. It seems remote from the (materially based) laws and needs of the 'world'.

The picture is complicated by the fact that poetry's raw material is language, the common property of everyday discourse.

Justifications take the form of statements like these from *Teaching Poetry in the Secondary School* (DES 1987), expressing 'an HMI view' and published at a crucial period in the formulation of the 1988 Education Reform Act that heralded the National Curriculum:

> Poetry matters because it is a central example of the use human beings make of words to explore and understand (p. 1),

> Poetry needs to be at the heart of work in English because of the quality of language at work on experience that it offers to us (p. 3);

and

> It is the place of poetry in English teaching to help us to restore to pupils a sense of exuberance and vitality in the acquisition of language and in the power and savour of words (ibid.).

These are fine words. Poetry has been given special attention because of its supposedly purifying quality, its universality, its restorative nature. But one could just as easily replace the word 'poetry' in each of these statements with 'literature'. One could even go as far as trying 'discussion', or any other form of lively discourse.

The mismatch between the ideal and the reality is, of course, very much on the minds of the composers of the HMI document; indeed, this must have been part of the reason for the publication of the document. No one would seek to justify the place of poetry in the curriculum in such eloquent style if he or she was assured of its place. And the fact of the matter is that the place of writing poetry is not assured.

The reality is described on the very next page (p. 4) of the booklet:

> The findings of specialist one-day visits and a number of full inspection reports show that poetry was at the centre of work in English for rather less than five per cent of the English lessons observed. The evidence is that, in national terms, poetry is frequently neglected and poorly provided for; its treatment is inadequate and superficial.

In this context, HMI are to be applauded for their spirited defence of poetry. The problem is that the defence is in the form of a rearguard action: it depends upon a view of poetry as moral and aesthetic arbiter, of poetry as one of the highest (if not *the* highest) form of verbal discourse, of poetry as the standard-bearer for the liberal arts. It seems to me that poetry has been asked to play too grand a role, and that it suffers accordingly. The mismatch between what is claimed for poetry and what is actually produced in the classroom makes for a tension that is not easily resolved.

Rather than claim too much for it, let us consider in more modest fashion what the case for poetry is. One contribution it can make – and one that is perceived by various commentators – is that it can raise awareness of language through the very fact of its status as an art. Drawing a frame around words to create a 'margin of silence' – even words that appear to be taken 'straight from life' – changes the way in which we look at them. To this extent we put ourselves in 'spectator' role and look at the relationship between the words, at their rhythmic, auditory and visual features, more than we would if they were unframed. As we become aware of their existence *as words*, so we increase our awareness of language in general. Whether or not this increases our ability to *use* language is not proven, nor is it the focus of our attention here. The important point to note is that poetry, by its very nature as an art form, does make us more aware of language *per se*. It thus fulfils one of the requirements of the national curriculum in English – knowledge about language – in a painless and indeed pleasurable way. One does not have to study language in order to increase awareness of it, or even to know more about it. Literature, and especially poetry, has been doing this in a quiet but effective way for some time.

Another way in which the place of poetry can be justified is much more complex, and is related to the argument of Chapter 4. There is something about the rhythmic nature of the poem that cannot be provided by any other part of the curriculum. We have tried to establish the centrality of rhythm to the definition of 'poem' in Chapters 2 and 4 in particular. The task here is different: it is to justify such an activity, practice and area of study.

Such a justification is possible, and in several respects. First – and most commonly – we hear poetry being justified for its contribution to the affective education of children in schools. In this respect, it is often presented as a counterweight to the 'intellectual' or practical pursuits that are deemed to take up most of the curriculum. Usually, this justification is linked to nothing as specific as rhythm: it is more often conceived in terms of the 'content' of poetry, its moods, its personal voice, its imaginative power – all of which we now recognize as being not only the province of poetry. We can be more specific about the relationship between poetry and feeling, but only if we attend to the rhythmic element more closely. Pound was perhaps nearest the mark in this area when he talked about the emotional content of a poem being carried in the cadence of the words, and the intellectual content in the images, i.e. the visual aspects of a poem appealing most strongly to the mind's eye, and the rhythmic patterning to the ear and the body. Being *moved*, then, might mean being moved to dance to the rhythm of a poem (or, of course, a piece of music), whether literally or metaphorically, and whether in saying it, writing it, singing, reading or hearing it.

Building a case for poetry from this angle puts it in the same camp as dance and music, two of the 'expressive arts'. Their justification is couched in terms of the shaping of experience – physical, aural and verbal – in conscious, pleasing and liberating ways. The difference between poetry and the rest of literature from this point of view is that poetry is closest to music and exists as a 'dance in words', to repeat Ted Hughes' part definition. There is plenty of evidence, too, to associate these three arts at the composing stage of poetry. This, from Christopher Middleton (1973: p. 53) will serve as an example:

> In my practice, the act of writing is often prepared by a distinctive moment in experience, a moment at which everything, including the conventional code (language) seems to be decomposing. This (Dada) moment is announced by the birth of a phrase, which has a distinct rhythm and resonance ... I become more than ordinarily receptive, once the process of decomposition has begun ... Mumbling, gnashing of teeth, clenching of fists, walking about, sudden raisings of the head, listenings. I excavate and assemble all sorts of fractions of language and experience, compelled, but also liberated, by the guiding rhythm.

Rhythmic fragments, lines and poems are 'equations for the emotions'; they communicate precisely because the perception of time – of things in relation to other things from a temporal point of view – is arranged to release some feeling. Our aesthetic experience is gauged against our 'inner metronome' – the heart – the conventional seat of the emotions, though we know that 'feeling' most often hits us in the stomach or somewhere else in the blood system.

This physicality, this dancing in the veins, is recorded in a poem by Bella Akhmadulina (quoted by Fred Sedgwick (1987)) in which the peculiar excitement of writing is likened to a disturbance in the state of the body, like a fever (in Rumens 1985: p. 58):

> I must be ill, of course. I've been shivering
> for three days now like a horse before the races

> . . . I was then so jerked about by
> fever, my words shook with it; my legs
> wobbled

Sedgwick also cites poems by Larkin, Heaney and Hughes to support his emerging thesis that the writing of a poem can be a disturbance – a positive, alienating and dangerous one, but one which creates poems in which animal imagery figures prominently. It is my contention, however, that more important than (though not unrelated to) the animal associations is the rhythmic nature of these poems, and the centrality of rhythm in the contemporary poetic. The key effect of rhythm is that, through its particular arrangements of words in time, it liberates feeling and spirit.

The network of rhythms present in a poem provide a further justification: that as well as releasing emotion, the poem acts as a preserver of felt experience. Through the action of repetition (and all its variations), time is 'defeated'. Rhythm is like an embalming fluid that keeps the experience preserved but which enables it to be recreated in some other time and context. This is about as close to the 'universality' sometimes claimed for poetry that we can get.

And for these last two reasons, at least, poetry gives pleasure. It can be a pleasure in the rhythmic patterning and/or in the savouring of words; it can be a pleasure in what is said; it can generate laughter as well as feeling. This exuberance and vitality isn't one we need to 'restore', as the HMI document has it; rather, it builds on the life and power that is in language. If we insist on seeing poetry as a restorative agent, we put too much on its shoulders and oppose it to the common language; this in itself is the product of a certain view of the relation of literature to everyday language: one that has inflated the claims of poetry and probably at the same time been partly the cause of the lack of enthusiasm for poetry.

The paradoxical nature and effect of the poem that is caught in the balance between order and disorder in rhythmic terms, in the iconoclastic and image-creating relationship, in the ambivalence towards time and in the relationship with 'everyday' language is evidenced too in the suggestion (made by Britton 1982: p. 16) that (in the poems he quotes to illustrate his argument), the need to write poetry arose 'because their created worlds were in danger of being disrupted' (p. 16). To take this point further, it seems to me that the disturbance a poem can bring – as evidenced in the Akhmadulina poem – is beneficial precisely because it forces a revaluation of the status quo. The 'stability' and 'equilibrium' thus established is not a conservative one, but one that registers a new state of feeling. This new state is arrived at by means of the relatively 'safe' operation of composing words within a frame.

Running alongside the view that poetry is 'restorative' is the notion (ibid. p. 18) that the effect of

> the regular beat of metrical language is to induce a mild hypnosis in the reader, a lulling of the critical and logical aspects of the mind: and that by this means, and

others, poets are able to make us *feel* the truth of some hypothesis which logical reasoning would refute.

Here, I would want to affirm this point, but again take it further. It is not only the 'regular beat' that induces such 'hypnosis', but other kinds of rhythm too; and no doubt different rhythms induce different kinds of states of mind and feeling. And the creation of a state of feeling need not take place at the expense or 'lulling' or suspension of the critical and logical faculties. Indeed, critical and emotively logical patterns can be created, enhancing the various perceptions and fusing feeling with critical insight. This heightened perception of order and of the sense of 'blood, spirit and intellect running together' is characteristic of poetry and music.

Another essay by Britton, 'Poetry and our pattern of culture' (1966; in 1982), does in fact take this particular argument further, and goes beyond anything I have argued in this book. It quotes Robert Graves:

> The nucleus of every poem worthy of the name is rhythmically formed in the poet's mind, during a trance-like suspension of his normal habits of thought, by the supra-logical reconciliation of conflicting emotional ideas. The poet learns to induce this trance in self-protection whenever he feels unable to resolve an emotional conflict by simple logic.

Britton glosses this position thus (1982: p. 28):

> The language of poetry, it seems to me, differs most from the language of prose statement in the power it possesses to represent, indeed to recreate, this two-sidedness. It does so in many ways – by its ambiguous use of words and syntax, by using rhythm and the corporeal qualities of words to give a sense that may be at variance with the paraphrasable meaning; by using images which may themselves bring contrary impulses into play.

This, then, is one more justification and explanation for the place of poetry in the curriculum, and one further aspect of the function of rhythm in poems: its ability to suggest flow and momentum at the same time as providing a patterning and shaping of experience, a setting up of expectation that is sometimes fulfilled and sometimes subverted. And whereas the ambiguity of words and syntax and that of imagery can be readily received by reading the poem on the page, the rhythmic effects of a poem are best experienced by reading the poem aloud, or by hearing it read aloud. All that has been said in this book about the line of poetry as the basic rhythmic unit has been mostly about the score and not so much about the performance. The rhythms only become fully realized in performance, and though the basic rhythmic frame remains the same from performance to performance, secondary aspects of the rhythmic identity of the poem, like pitch, tempo and inflection, come into play once the poem is 'returned' to speech.

This emphasis on the rhythmic nature of poetry is not to diminish the effect of metaphor and other kinds of imagery, but part of its intention is to get this powerful function of poetic language into perspective, rather than being 'at the centre of poetic expression' (DES 1987: p. 21). Figurative language is a secondary feature of poetry because the nature of language is spoken and auditory, dialogic and rhythmical; and because metaphors are primarily visual and the product of the imagination. It operates in fields other than poetry and with great effect. Above all, its transformational energy helps us to see links between phenomena that ordinarily we would take for granted or are blind to. It can operate indirectly, revealing truths in delightful and surprising ways.

Undue emphasis on the figurative aspect of poetic expression tends to set poetry apart from other kinds of discourse. Typical of this position is that of Hillyer (1960), quoted by Ried (1987: p. 477), in which the poetic temperament is projected from a notion of the nature of poetry (which nevertheless is said to be 'indefinable'). The poetic temperament is:

> that faculty that feels the most ordinary events as something wonderful and interesting, the most ordinary routine of life as something beautiful and significant. [The poet] uses the same words as everybody else, but in rarer and more suggestive combinations. To evoke metaphor: the poet is the stained-glass window that transmits sunlight just as ordinary windows do, but colors it as it passes through.

This transformational quality has been enshrined by Day Lewis (1947: p. 17) thus:

> . . . the image is the constant in all poetry, and every poem is itself an image. Trends come and go, diction alters, metrical fashions change, even the elemental subject-matter may change out of all recognition: but metaphor remains, the life-principle of poetry, the poet's chief test and glory.

Day Lewis supplements this formulation with further reference to Coleridge, asking (p. 19) whether Coleridge himself should have the last word:

> Images, however beautiful . . . do not of themselves characterize the poet. They become proofs of original genius only as far as they are modified by a predominant passion; or by associated thoughts or images awakened by that passion.

Even if we accept the Vygotskian perception that speech is a symbolic system and that writing is a second order symbolic system (and that play is a way of developing symbolism – see Vygotsky 1978: p. 108ff), we are acknowledging the power of language as symbol but not confining this symbolic operation to poetry (or more broadly, literature).

It follows from much of what has been said in this book, and particularly in this last chapter, that the coupling of feeling and form is unhelpful as an antithesis. The polarity is framed in the following way. On the one hand, there are those who argue that poetry is best generated by creating an atmosphere or by enriching the sensibilities of the pupils in a classroom or school. The argument follows that by creating a fertile soil, the individual seeds will flourish. The soil is nourished by readings of poems, by having books of poems readily at hand, by displaying the work of children, by being aware of the poetic possibilities in language and attuning everyone to these possibilities; by forging the connection between 'voice' and poetry. With this approach, the transformation from reading to writing poetry takes place more by a process of osmosis than of application.

On the other hand, there are those who argue for a more rigorous approach to poetry: one that is grounded in poetic form. Their argument runs like this: poetry is a distinctive kind of discourse. We should move from the primitive forms of poetry to more complex forms, exploring models and ways of writing that will give access to feeling. Concentration should be on the technique and on the subject of the poem, rather than on the feeling, because this is the way that good poetry reveals itself. This is an art-form, and if it is worth bothering with at all, it is worth doing well.

If this book has seemed to argue the case for the second of these approaches more than for the first, it is only in an attempt to balance the approaches overall after a period in which the former approach has held sway. It is also an attempt to argue for the place of poetry in the curriculum at a time when it seems threatened by more pragmatic and more assessment-driven forms of education.

In truth, the two approaches (which I have characterized as such for dialectical purposes) are complementary. The caricature of the emotionally sensitive and pumped-up class is as bad as that of the mindless form-obsessed approach, and there is a middle ground which combines the best of both approaches. Forms are indeed 'empty structures' unless they are infused with life and imaginative energy; 'expression' is chaotic unless it takes some kind of shape. The secret, it seems to me, is to tread that delicate line between the public forms that have gathered associations and functions, not only in our society but across the world, and the private perceptions, the fresh revaluations of language that occur when an individual grapples with language and experience, with the effort of getting thoughts and feelings into words. And we must not be distracted by the high-sounding claims made for poetry as we practise it in the classroom: our attention must be focused on the job in hand. Wei T'ai's advice, quoted in Chapter 7, is echoed by David Holbrook (1981: p. 40);

> In writing poetry, one communicates, perhaps, a kind of language and a kind of form ... but then what one gets is a kind of content, a way of approaching experience ...

What we must not lose sight of is the connection between the kinds of form and content that have tended to give expression to private and personal feelings and the more public forms and channels that poetry can inhabit. As Michael Rosen suggests in *I See a Voice* (1981), poems can be seen as parts of conversations and as elements in argument; they can 'become the most political of actions, a moving outward of the individual consciousness to find new forms and new people, to explore, discover and change the world' (Searle 1963). In these senses, poetry reaffirms its connection with rhetoric and with the life of language in a democracy.

Being aware of the 'public forms' also means exploring and enjoying what has already been written. That exploration of literature has only been implicit in this book, which has focused more on the composition and production of poetry than on the reception and response to it. This is, however, merely a matter of emphasis, because reading as a writer and writing as a reader are complementary positions: both writing and reading feed off each other. This applies as much – if not more – to teachers as to pupils, as is suggested in *Teaching Poetry in the Secondary School* (1987: p. 29):

> The close connection between reading and writing poetry demonstrates the proper seriousness of the matter [of poetry], as ideas and feelings are wrought into expressive form. Though tactful, sensitive and positive, the teacher must not receive pupils' work with easy and sentimental praise. Pupils as writers need the benefit of clear and frank appraisal, an expectation that they will rework ideas in sections of their writing, and plenty of time and encouragement to do so. It follows that teachers need to be sure of their judgements, to be widely read in poetry themselves, and perhaps to be engaged in the business of writing themselves alongside their pupils from time to time.

Thus it becomes 'not . . . a matter of chance, but of entitlement' (ibid. p. 33) that literature is present to developing writers and readers.

This book attempts to bring the writing of poetry to the edge of reading literature; to a place from which the reading of poetry seems a natural – and indeed, already taken – step. There is no grand chronological plan behind dealing with the writing of poetry first: the two practices go hand in hand, though it may be that committing oneself in writing to a theme or style gives an extra incentive to finding out how others have dealt with the same theme or style. The general principle embodied here is applicable to reading poetry too, as expressed by Alberta Turner (1982):

> To begin, I would select poems of the highest quality, strongly emotional, rhetori- cally simple, conversational, fairly modern in diction and universal in theme.

For all my reservations about the claims of universality and the narrowness of a poetry based on emotion, this seems as good a place to start as any. If this book has suggested some ways of solving some of the problems that beset poetry – whether they are to do with teaching methods, attitudes, understanding of poetic forms, or realignments of priorities in our view of poetry – it will have been of some use. But the 'solutions' are far less satisfying and interesting than the problems – or the poems themselves.

References and select bibliography

Abbs, P. (1975), 'Poetry as process' in *The Use of English*, vol. 26, no. 4, Summer 1975.

Abbs, P. (1982), *English within the Arts*. London, Hodder and Stoughton.

Abbs, P. and Richardson, J. (1990), *The Forms of Poetry*. Cambridge, Cambridge University Press.

Adams, N. (1969), 'Painting and poetry' in *English in Education*, vol. 3, no. 2, Summer 1969.

Alvarez, A. (1962), *The New Poetry*. Harmondsworth, Penguin.

Andrews, R. (1978), 'Poetry and the impossible' in *The Use of English*, vol. 30, no. 1, Autumn 1978.

Andrews, R. (1983), *Into Poetry*. London, Ward Lock Educational.

Andrews, R. (1989), 'Beyond "voice" in poetry' in *English in Education*, vol. 23, no. 3, Autumn 1989.

Andrews, R. (1990), 'Another look at poetry anthologies' in *The Use of English*, vol. 41, no. 2, Spring 1990.

Andrews, R. (1991), *Poetry* (Macmillan English Modules). London, Macmillan.

Andrews, R. (ed.) (1989). *Narrative and Argument*. Milton Keynes, Open University Press.

Andrews, R. and Bentley, I (ed.) (1987), *Poetry Horizons*, vols. 1 & 2. London, Bell and Hyman.

Armstrong, C. (1985). 'Tracking the Muse: The Composing Processes of Poets', unpublished Ph.D. thesis, University of California, Santa Barbara.

Arnold, M. (1960), 'The study of poetry' in *Essays in Criticism: second series* (ed. Littlewood, S. R.). London, Macmillan.

Ashton, P. and Marigold, D. (1987). 'Poetry 1–3: Tennis in a thunderstorm?' in Hunt *et al.* (1987).

Atkinson, J. (1985), 'How children read poems at different ages' in *English in Education*, vol. 19, no. 1, Spring 1985.

Attridge, D. (1982), *The Rhythms of English Poetry*. Harlow, Longman.

Auden, W. H. (1975), *The Dyer's Hand & Other Essays*. London, Faber & Faber.

Bakhtin, M. M. (1981), *The Dialogic Imagination*. Austin, University of Texas Press.

Bakhtin, M. M. (1986), *Speech Genres and Other Late Essays*. Austin, University of Texas Press.

Balaam, J. and Merrick, B. (n.d.), *Exploring Poetry 5–8*. Sheffield, National Association for the Teaching of English.

Bann, S. (1967). *Concrete Poetry: An International Anthology*. London, London Magazine Editions.

Barrell, J. (1988), *Poetry, Language and Politics*. Manchester, Manchester University Press.

Barrs, M. (1987). 'Mapping the world' in *English in Education*, vol. 21, no. 1, Spring 1987.

Barry, P. (1978), 'How not to read a poem' in *The Use of English*, vol. 29, no. 3, Summer 1978.

Baudelaire, C. (1961). *Selected Verse* (ed. Scarfe, Francis). Harmondsworth, Penguin.

Beckett, J. (1965), *The Keen Edge: An Analysis of Poems by Adolescents*. London, Blackie and Sons.

Bennett, S. *et al.* (n.d.). *West Indian Poetry*. London, ILEA English Centre.

Benton, M. and P. (1987–8). *Touchstones I–V* (revised ed.). London, Hodder & Stoughton.

Benton, M. *et al.* (1988). *Young Readers Responding to Poems*. London, Routledge.

Berger, J. and Mohr, J. (1980). *Another Way of Telling*. London, Writers' and Readers' Publishing Co-op.

Berry, C. (1974). *Voice and the Actor*. London, Harrap.

Berry, F. (1962). *Poetry and the Physical Voice*. London, Routledge & Kegan Paul.

Black, E. L. (ed.) (1966), *Nine Modern Poets*. London, Macmillan.

Brik, A. (1927), 'Contributions to the study of verse language', C. H. Severens (trans.) in Matejka and Pomorska (eds.), *Readings in Russian Poetics*, 1971.

Bolton, E. J. (1966), *Verse Writing in Schools*. Oxford, Pergamon.

Bowra, C. M. (1966). *Poetry and Politics 1900–1960*. Cambridge, Cambridge University Press.

Brecht, B. (1976), *Poems 1913–1956*. London, Eyre Methuen.

Britton, J. (1953), 'Words and the imagination' in Britton (1982).

Britton, J. (1954), 'Evidence of improvement in poetic judgement' in *British Journal of Psychology*, vol. 45, no. 3, pp. 196–208.

Britton, J. (1958). 'Reading and writing poetry' in Britton (1982).

Britton, J. (1966). 'Poetry and our pattern of culture' in Britton (1982).

Britton, J. (1982). *Prospect and Retrospect* (ed. Pradl, Gordon). Montclair, N. J., Boynton/ Cook.

Britton, J. N. *et al.* (1973), *The Development of Writing Abilities, 11–16*. London, Macmillan.

Brooks, C. (1947). *The Well-Wrought Urn*. New York, Harcourt and Brace.

Browning, Elizabeth Barrett (1983), *Selected Poems* (ed. Hicks, Malcolm). Manchester, Carcanet Press.

Brownjohn, S. (1980). *Does it Have to Rhyme?* London, Hodder & Stoughton.

Brownjohn, S. (1982). *What Rhymes with 'Secret'?* London, Hodder & Stoughton.

Brownjohn, S. (1990), *The Ability to Name Cats*. London, Hodder & Stoughton.

Brownjohn, S. and A. (1985), *Meet and Write 1, 2, & 3*. London, Hodder & Stoughton.

Brumfit, C. J. and Carter, R. A. (1986), *Literature and Language Teaching*. Oxford, Oxford University Press.

Burton, S. (1969), 'Approaches to creative writing' in *English in Education*, vol. 3, no. 3, Autumn 1969.

Calkins, L. M (1986), *The Art of Teaching Writing*. London, Heinemann Education.

Calthrop, K. and Ede, J. (1984), *Not 'Daffodils' Again! Teaching Poetry 9–13*. York, Longman Resources Unit.

Carver, R. (1988), *In a Marine Light*. London, Pan Books.

Carver, R. (1989), *A New Path to the Waterfall*. London, Collins Harvill.

Chambers, H. (1978), 'A pot-pourri of poetry matters' in *The Use of English*, vol. 30, no. 1, Autumn 1978.

Clare, J. (1967), *Selected Poems and Prose of John Clare* (chosen and edited by Robinson, E. and Summerfield, G.). Oxford, Oxford University Press.

Clegg, A. B. (1964), *The Excitement of Writing*. London, Chatto & Windus.

Cook, H. C. (1912), *Perse Playbooks* 1–6. Cambridge.

Cook, S. (1978), 'Seeing your meaning' in *The Use of English*, vol. 30, no. 1, Autumn 1978.

Corbett, P. and Moses, B. (1986), *Catapults and Kingfishers*. Oxford, Oxford University Press.

Cosman, C., *et al.* (1979), *The Penguin Book of Woman Poets*. Harmondsworth, Penguin.

Couzyn, J. (1985), *The Bloodaxe Book of Contemporary Women Poets*. Newcastle, Bloodaxe.

Cromley, M. (1976), in *Journal of Reading*, vol. 19, no. 4 (January 1976).

Culler, J. (1975), *Structuralist Poetics*. London, Routledge & Kegan Paul.

Cullingford, C. (1979), 'Children and poetry' in *English in Education*, vol. 13, no. 2, Summer 1979.

Danby, J. F. (1940), *Approach to Poetry*. London, Heinemann.

Davie, D. (1967), *Purity of Diction in English Verse*. London, Routledge & Kegan Paul.

Davies, J. (1980), 'Tactics with poetry: 2' in *The Use of English*, vol. 31, no. 3, Summer 1980.

Day Lewis, C. (1947), *The Poetic Image*. London, Jonathan Cape.

De Sola Pinto, V. and Rodway, A. (1957), *The Common Muse*. London, Chatto & Windus.

Deller, B. (1981), 'Forms of poetry' in *English in Education*, vol. 15, no. 3, Autumn 1981.

Department of Education and Science (1975), *A Language for Life* (the Bullock Report). London, HMSO.

Department of Education and Science (1987), *Teaching Poetry in the Secondary School: An HMI View*. London, HMSO.

Department of Education and Science (1988), *An Inquiry into the Teaching of English* (the Kingman Report). London, HMSO.

Department of Education and Science (1989), *English for Ages 5 to 16: proposals of the Secretary of State for Education and Science and the Secretary of State for Wales* (the Cox Report). York, National Curriculum Council.

Dias, P. (1986), 'Making sense of poetry: patterns of response among Canadian and British secondary school pupils' in *English in Education*, vol. 20, no. 2, Summer 1986.

Dias, P. and Hayhoe, M. (1988), *Developing Response to Poetry*. Milton Keynes, Open University Press.

Dombey, H. (1969), 'Creative writing in the junior school' in *English in Education*, vol. 3, no. 3, Autumn 1969.

Druce, R. (1965), *The Eye of Innocence*. Leicester, Brockhampton Press.

Dunn, D. (1974), 'I am a Cameraman' in *Love or Nothing*. London, Faber & Faber.

Elbow, P. (1973), *Writing without Teachers*. London, Oxford University Press.

Eliot, T. S. (1933), *The Use of Poetry and the Use of Criticism*. London, Faber & Faber.

Eliot, V. (1971), *The Waste Land: A Facsimile & Transcript*. London, Faber & Faber.

Evans, T. (1982), *Teaching English*. London, Croom Helm.

Fairfax, J. and Moat, J. (1981), *The Way to Write*. London, Elm Tree Books.

Fenollosa, E. (1936), *The Chinese Written Character as a Medium for Poetry* (ed. Pound, E.). San Francisco, City Lights Books.

Finnegan, R. (1978), *The Penguin Book of Oral Poetry*. London, Allen Lane.

Forrest-Thomson, V. (1978), *Poetic Artifice*. Manchester, Manchester University Press.

Fox, G. and Merrick, B. (1981), '36 things to do with a poem' in *Children's Literature in Education*, no. 12, Spring 1981.

Freer, A. (1969), 'Creative writing and the fertile image' in *English in Education*, vol. 3, no. 2, Summer 1969.

Frye, N. (1963), *The Well-Tempered Critic*. Bloomington, Indiana University Press.

Gardner, H. (1949), *The Art of T. S. Eliot*. London, Cresset Press.

Garnett, D. (1989), 'Coxed to Victory?' in *English in Education*, vol. 23, no. 2. Summer 1989.

Genette, G. (1980), *Narrative Discourse*. Ithaca, Cornell University Press.

Genette, G. (1988), *Narrative Discourse Revisited*. Ithaca, Cornell University Press.

Gilbert, P. (1989), *Writing, Schooling and Deconstruction*. London, Routledge.

Graves, D. (1983), *Writing: Children and Teachers at Work*. London, Heinemann.

Greenwell, A. and Peek, M. (1984), *Open the Door*. London, John Murray.

Guillén, N. (1972), *Patria o Muerte! The Great Zoo and Other Poems*. New York, Monthly Review Press.

Gutteridge, D. (1988), *The Dimension of Delight: A Study of Children's Verse-Writing, Ages 11–13*. London, Ontario, The Althouse Press.

Hale, T. (1971), 'Teaching poetry through rock music' in *English in Education*, vol. 5, no. 1, Spring 1971.

Hamburger, M. (ed.) (1972), *East German Poetry*. Manchester, Carcanet Press.

Harcourt, R. (1974), 'Shaping poems' in *The Use of English*, vol. 25, no. 4, Summer 1974.

Harvey, J. (1969), 'A writing lesson' in *English in Education*, vol. 3, no. 3, Autumn 1969.

Hayhoe, M. and Parker, S. (1988), *Words Large as Apples*. Cambridge, Cambridge University Press.

Heaney, S. and Hughes, T. (1982), *The Rattle Bag*. London, Faber & Faber.

Henson, S. (1980), 'Tactics with poetry: 1' in *The Use of English*, vol. 31, no. 3, Summer 1980.

Heylen, J. and Jellett, C. (1987), *Rattling in the Wind*. Cambridge, Cambridge University Press.

Hidden, N. and Hollins, A. (1978), *Many People, Many Voices*. London, Hutchinson.

Hillyer, R. S. (1960), *In Pursuit of Poetry*. New York, McGraw-Hill.

Holbrook, D. (1981). 'Ten year old poets' in *The Use of English*, vol. 33, no. 1, Autumn 1981.

Hollander, J. (1989), *Rhyme's Reason*. New Haven, Yale University Press.

Holub, M. (1984), *On the Contrary*. Newcastle, Bloodaxe Books.

Hooke, R. (1665), *Micrographia*.

Hourd, M. (1949), *The Education of the Poetic Spirit*. London, Heinemann.

Hourd, M. and Cooper, G. (1959), *Coming Into Their Own*. London, Heinemann.

Howatson, M. C. (ed.) (1989), *The Oxford Companion to Classical Literature*. Oxford, Oxford University Press.

Hughes, T. (ed.) (1963), *Here Today*. London, Hutchinson.

Hughes, T. (1967), *Poetry in the Making*. London, Faber & Faber.

Hughes, T. (1970), *Crow*. London, Faber & Faber.

Hughes, T. (1976), *Season Songs*. London, Faber & Faber.

Hulme, T. E. (1962), *Further Speculations*. Lincoln, Nebraska, University of Nebraska Press.

Hunt, P. *et al.* (1987), *The English Curriculum: Poetry*. London, ILEA English Centre.

Isherwood, C. (1939), *Goodbye to Berlin*. London, The Hogarth Press.

Jackson, D. (1979), 'Process in action: a sixth form approach to Seamus Heaney' in *English in Education*, vol, 13, no. 3, Autumn 1979.

Jackson, D. (1982), *Continuity in English*. London, Methuen.

Jackson, D. (1986), 'Poetry and the speaking voice' in *English in Education*, vol. 20, no. 2, Summer 1986.

Jenkinson, A. J. (1940), *What Do Boys and Girls Read?* London, Methuen.

Jones, N. (1983), 'On anthologies' in *The Use of English*, vol. 34, no. 1, Autumn 1983.

Jones, R. (1986), *One World Poets*. London, Heinemann.

Joubert, J. (1978), 'Composing music for poetry' in *The Use of English*, vol. 30, no. 1, Autumn 1978.

Keats, J. (1917), *The Poetical Works of John Keats* (ed. Buxton Forman, H.). London, Oxford University Press.

Kelly, M. (1969), 'Approaches to poetry using translations' in *English in Education*, vol. 3, no. 1, Spring 1969.

Kelly, M. (1973), 'Some approaches to poetry for students of English' in *English in Education*, vol. 7, no. 1, Spring 1973.

Kermode, F. (1990), *Poetry, Narrative, History*. Oxford, Basil Blackwell.

Kingsley, B. (1978), 'Dramatic poetry' in *The Use of English*, vol. 30, no. 1, Autumn 1978.

Koch, K. (1970), *Wishes, Lies and Dreams*. New York, Harper & Row.

Koch, K. (1974), *Rose, Where Did You Get That Red?* New York, Random House.

Langdon, M. (1961), *Let the Children Write*. London, Longman.

Langer, S. (1953), *Feeling and Form*. New York, Schribner's.

Langer, S. (1957), *Philosophy in a New Key*. Cambridge, Mass., Harvard University Press.

Leach, E. (1970), *Lévi-Strauss*. London, Fontana.

Leech, G. N. (1969), *A Linguistic Guide to English Poetry*. Harlow, Longman.

Leggett, J. and Moger, R. (n.d.). *Yesterday Today Tomorrow*. London, ILEA English Centre.

Lester, J. (1969), *Search for a New Land: History of Subjective Experience*. New York, Dial Press.

Lotman, Y. (1976), *Analysis of the Poetic Text*. Ann Arbor, Ardis.

Lowell, R. (1970), *Notebook*. London, Faber & Faber.

Mallarmé, S. (1886–95), 'Crisis in Poetry' in *Selected Prose, Poems, Essays and Letters*, trans. Bradford Cook. Baltimore, Johns Hopkins University Press, 1956.

Mallarmé, S. (1897), *Un Coup de Dès* (translated 1956 by Aldan. Daisy).

McEwen, P. (1989), 'Cooperative poetry' in *Reading Teacher*, vol. 42, no. 7, March 1989.

McGough, R. (1981), *Strictly Private*. London, Kestrel.

McKendy, T. (1987), 'Arguing about taste: an introduction to poetry' in *English in Education*, vol. 21, no. 3, Autumn 1987.

Mapanje, J. and White, L. (eds.) (1983), *Oral Poetry from Africa*. Harlow, Longman.

Mathieson, M. (1980), 'The problem of poetry' in *The Use of English*, vol. 31, no. 2.

Mayer, P. (ed.) (1978), *Alphabetical and Letter Poems*. London, Menard Press.

Merrick, B. (1989), *Talking with Charles Causley*. Sheffield, National Association for the Teaching of English.

Middleton, C. (1973) in *Agenda* (Supplement on rhythm: from America), vol. 11, nos. 2–3, Spring-Summer 1973.

Middleton, S. C. (ed.) (1989), *Ostinato* 2: a magazine of jazz related poetry. London, Ostinato.

Mitchell, A. (1982), *For Beauty Douglas: Collected Poems 1953–1979*. London, Allison & Busby.

Moffett, J. (1968), *Teaching the Universe of Discourse*. Boston, Houghton Mifflin.

Moffett, J. (1981), *Active Voice*. New Jersey, Boynton/Cook.

Morgan, E. (1968), *The Second Life*. Edinburgh, Edinburgh University Press.

Morgan, E. (1972), *Instamatic Poems*. London, Ian McKelvie.

Morgan, E. (1973), *From Glasgow to Saturn*. Cheadle, Carcanet Press.

Morgan, E. (1974), *Essays*. Cheadle, Carcanet New Press.

Morgan, E. (1977), *The New Divan*. Manchester, Carcanet Press.

Morgan, E. (1979), *Star Gate*. Glasgow, Third Eye Centre.

Morgan, E. (1982), *Poems of Thirty Years*. Manchester, Carcanet Press.

Morgan, E. (1988), *Themes on a Variation*. Manchester, Carcanet Press.

Murray, G. (1975), 'Poetry in the classroom' in *English in Education*, vol. 9, no. 3, Winter 1975.

Nash, C. (1980), 'Metre for all?' in *The Use of English*, vol. 31, no. 2, Spring 1980.

Neruda, P. (1970), *Selected Poems*. London, Jonathan Cape.

Nicholls, J. (1985), *Magic Mirror*. London, Faber and Faber.

O'Malley, R. (1969), 'Creative writing in the schools' in *English in Education*, vol. 3, no. 3, Autumn 1969

Orme, D. (ed.) (1987), *The Windmill Book of Poetry*. London, Heinemann.

Paulin, T. (ed.) (1986), *The Faber Book of Political Verse*. London, Faber & Faber.

Paz, O. (1974), *Alternating Current*. London, Wildwood House.

Paz, O. *et al.* (1979), *Renga*. Harmondsworth, Penguin.

Phillips, T. (1971), 'Poetry in the junior school' in *English in Education*, vol. 5, no. 3, Winter 1971.

Pirrie, J. (1987), *On Common Ground*. London, Hodder & Stoughton.

Plath, S. (1977), 'A Comparison' in *Johnny Panic and the Bible of Dreams*. London, Faber & Faber.

Popa, V. (1980), *The Golden Apple* (chosen and translated by Andrew Harvey & Anne Pennington). London, Anvil Press.

Pound, E. (1912), *Ripostes of Ezra Pound*. London, Stephen Swift.

Pound, E. (1951a), *The Letters of Ezra Pound 1907–1941* (ed. Paige, D. D.). London, Faber & Faber.

Pound, E. (1951b), *The ABC of Reading*. London, Faber & Faber.

Pound, E. (1954), *Literary Essays of Ezra Pound*. London, Faber & Faber.

Powell, B. (1968), *English through Poetry Writing*. London, Heinemann.

Powell, N. (1974), 'Is there a poetry of rock?' in *The Use of English*, vol. 26, no. 2, Winter 1974.

Powell, N. (1979), 'Making poems' in *The Use of English*, vol. 30, no. 2, Spring 1979.

Pratt, M. L. (1977), *Towards a Speech Act Theory of Literary Discourse*. Bloomington, Indiana University Press.

Preen, D. (1990), 'English for ages 5 to 16: A document for hard times' in *The Use of English*, vol. 41, no. 2, Spring 1990.

Preminger, A. *et al.* (1986), *The Princeton Handbook of Poetic Terms*. Princeton, NJ, Princeton University Press.

Press, J. (1969), *A Map of Modern English Verse*. Oxford, Oxford University Press.

Protherough, R. (1978), 'When in doubt, write a poem' in *English in Education*, vol. 12, no. 1, Spring 1978.

Protherough, R. (1984), *Developing Response to Fiction*. Milton Keynes, Open University Press.

Raine, C. (1979), *A Martian Sends a Postcard Home*. Oxford, Oxford University Press.

Raychaudhuri, S. and Read, R. (1990), *Bengali Poetry/English Poetry*. London, Kavita Productions.

Richards, I. A. (1929), *Practical Criticism*. London, Routledge & Kegan Paul.

Ricoeur, P. (1984), *Time and Narrative*, vol. 1. Chicago, Chicago University Press.

Ricoeur, P. (1985), *Time and Narrative*, vol. 2. Chicago, Chicago University Press.

Ricoeur, P. (1988), *Time and Narrative*, vol. 3. Chicago, Chicago University Press.

Ried, P. E. (1987), 'The Boylston professor in the twentieth century' in *Quarterly Journal of Speech*, vol. 73, no. 4, November 1987.

Riffaterre, M. (1978), *Semiotics of Poetry*, Bloomington, Indiana University Press.

Robbins, S. (1970), 'The writing of poetry – one way in' in *English in Education*, vol. 4, no. 1, Spring 1970.

Roberts, M. (1982), *The Faber Book of Modern Verse*. London, Faber and Faber.

Rosen, M. (1981), *I See a Voice*. London, Thames TV/Hutchinson.

Rosen, M. (1985), *The Kingfisher Book of Children's Poetry*. London, Kingfisher.

Rosen, M. (1989), *Did I Hear You Write?* London, Deutsch.

Rosen, M. and Jackson, D. (1984), *Speaking to You*. London, Macmillan.

Rothenburg, J. (1972), *Shaking the Pumpkin: Traditional poetry of the Indian North Americas*. New York, Doubleday.

Rothstein, A. (1979), *Words and Pictures*. New York, Amphoto.

Rumens, C. (ed.) (1985), *Making for the Open*. London, Chatto and Windus.

Scholes, R. (1974), *Structuralism in Literature: An Introduction*. New Haven, Yale University Press.

Searle, C. (1963), *This New Season*. London, Calder and Boyars.

Sedgwick, F. (1987), 'The green fire: poems about the beginning of poems' in *Cambridge Journal of Education*, vol. 17, no. 2.

Shaw, M. A. (1982). 'Word and image – mixed ability poetry?' in *English in Education*, vol. 16, no. 3, Autumn 1982.

Shonagon, S. (1971), *The Pillow Book of Sei Shonagon*. Harmondsworth, Penguin.

Sidney, Sir P. (1987), 'The Defence of Poesy' in *Selected Writings* (ed. Dutton, Richard). Manchester, Carcanet Press.

Smith, B. H. (1968), *Poetic Closure*. Chicago, University of Chicago Press.

Solzhenitsyn, A. (1973), *Stories and Prose Poems*. Harmondsworth, Penguin.

Stankiewicz, E. (1961), 'Poetic and non-poetic language in their interrelation' in Davie *et al.*, *Poetics: Papers Read at the First International Conference of Work-in-Progress Devoted to the Problems of Poetics*.

Stevens, W. (1953), *Selected Poems*. London, Faber & Faber.

Stibbs, A. (1983), 'Teaching poetry legally' in *English in Education*, vol. 17, no. 3, Autumn 1983.

Stibbs, A. and Newbould, A. (1983), *Exploring Texts*. London, Ward Lock Educational.

Stibbs, A. *et al.* (n.d.). *Natepack 1: Poetry*. Sheffield, National Association for the Teaching of English.

Styles, M. (1984). *I Like That Stuff.* Cambridge, Cambridge University Press.

Styles, M. (1986), *You'll Love This Stuff.* Cambridge, Cambridge University Press.

Styles, M. and Triggs, P. (1988), *Poetry 0–16*. London, Books for Keeps.

Sukhbir (n.d), 'Still Life' in *Indian Poetry Today*, vol. 1, New Delhi, Indian Council for Public Relations.

Summerfield, G. (ed.) (1968), *Voices 1–3*. Harmondsworth, Penguin.

Summerfield, G. (1970), *Creatures Moving.* Harmondsworth, Penguin.

Summerfield, G. (1978), 'Introducing the emblems of Ian Hamilton Finlay' in *The Use of English*, vol. 30, no. 1, Autumn 1978.

Summerfield, G. and Andrews, R. (1983), *Words*, vols. 1–3. London, Cassell.

Summerfield, G. and S. (1986), *Texts and Contexts*. New York, Random House.

Swanger, D. (1974), *The Poem as Process*. New York, Harcourt, Brace, Jovanovitch.

Tarleton, R. (1983), 'Children's thinking and poetry' in *English in Education*, vol. 17, no. 3, Autumn 1983.

Terkel, S. (1977), *Working*. Harmondsworth, Penguin.

Thompson, D. (1976), 'Poems before print' in *The Use of English*, vol. 27, no. 2, Spring 1976.

Todorov, T. (1982), *Theories of the Symbol*. Oxford, Basil Blackwell.

Tomlinson, C. (ed.) (1972), *William Carlos Williams* (Penguin Critical Anthologies). Harmondsworth, Penguin.

Travers, D. M. M. (1982), 'Problems in writing about poetry, and some solutions' in *English in Education*, vol. 16, no. 2, Autumn 1982.

Trotter, D. (1984), *The Making of the Reader: Language and Subjectivity in Modern American, English and Irish Poetry*. London, Macmillan.

Tunnicliffe, S. (1984), *Poetry Experience*. London, Methuen.

Turner, A. (1982), 'Teaching poetry writing in secondary school' in *English Journal*, vol. 71, no. 5, September 1982.

Valéry, P. (1938), 'Poetry and Abstract Thought' in *The Art of Poetry*, trans. Denise Folliot, *Collected Works of Paul Valéry*, ed. Jackson Matthews. New York, Pantheon Books, Bollingen Series, 1958.

Voloshinov, V. (1983), 'Discourse in life and discourse in poetry: questions of sociological poetics' in *Bakhtin Schools Papers* (ed. Shukman, A.), Russian Poetics in Translation, no. 10. Oxford, RPT Publications.

Vonnegut, K. (1970), *Slaughterhouse-Five*. London, Jonathan Cape.

Voznesensky, A. (1980), *Nostalgia for the Present*. Oxford, Oxford University Press.

Vygotksy, L. (1986), *Thought and Language*. Boston, MIT Press.

Wade, B. (1975), 'Haiku: the great leveller' in *English in Education*, vol. 9, no. 2, Summer 1975.

Walsh, J. H. (1973), *Presenting Poetry*. London, Heinemann.

Warnke, F. J. (1961), *European Metaphysical Poetry*. New Haven, Yale University Press.

Whitcombe, V. (1977), 'Poetry in prison' in *The Use of English*, vol. 29, no. 1, Autumn 1977.

Williams, E. (1967), *An Anthology of Concrete Poetry*. New York, Something Else Press.

Wilson, D. G. (ed.) (1975), *New Ships*. Oxford, Oxford University Press.

Wilson, R. (1982), 'Did you ever see a poet?' in *The Use of English*, vol. 34, no. 1, Autumn 1982.

Winick, S. D. (1974), *Rhythm: an annotated bibliography*. Metuchen, N.J., The Scarecrow Press.

Wollman, M. (ed.) (1957), *Ten Twentieth Century Poets*. London, Harrap.

Wood, F. (1975), 'An extended poetry workshop' in *The Use of English*, vol. 26, no. 4, Summer 1975.

Woodhead C. (1984), *Nineteenth and Twentieth Century Verse*. Oxford, Oxford University Press.

Wooding, C. R. (1961), *Politics in the Poetry of Coleridge*. Madison, Wisc., University of Wisconsin Press.

Yarlott, G. and Harpin, W. (1970–1), '1000 Responses to English Literature' in *Educational Research*, vol. 13, nos. 1 & 2.

Young, D. (1975), 'Shaping a poem' in *English in Education*, vol. 9, no. 3, Winter 1975.

Index